D0325813

EVIDENCE ON HER OWN BEHALF

New Feminist Perspectives Series

General Editor: Rosemarie Tong, Davidson College

EVIDENCE ON HER OWN BEHALF

Women's Narrative as Theological Voice

Elizabeth A. Say

Rowman & Littlefield Publishers, Inc.

PR 830
.F45
S29
1990

022345508

ROWMAN & LITTLEFIELD PUBLISHERS, INC.

Published in the United States of America
by Rowman & Littlefield Publishers, Inc.
8705 Bollman Place, Savage, Maryland 20763

Copyright © 1990 by Rowman & Littlefield Publishers, Inc.

All rights reserved. No part of this publication may
be reproduced, stored in a retrieval system, or transmitted
in any form or by any means, electronic, mechanical,
photocopying, recording, or otherwise, without the prior
permission of the publisher.

British Cataloging in Publication Information Available

Library of Congress Cataloging-in-Publication Data

Say, Elizabeth A.
    Evidence on her own behalf : women's narrative as
theological voice / Elizabeth A. Say.
        p.   cm. — (New feminist perspectives series)
    Includes bibliographical references and index.
    1. English fiction—Women authors—History and
criticism—Theory, etc.   2. Sayers, Dorothy L. (Dorothy
Leigh), 1893-1957—Criticism and interpretation.
3. English fiction—Women authors—History and criticism.
4.   Feminism and literature—Great Britain.   5. Religion
and literature—Great Britain.   6. Women and literature—
Great Britain.   7. Women—Education—Great Britain.
8. Feminism—Religious aspects.   9. Women—Religious
life.   10. Narration (Rhetoric)   I. Title.   II. Series.
PR830.F45S29   1990
823.009'9287—dc20   90-46391 CIP

ISBN 0-8476-7621-8 (cloth : alk. paper)

5   4   3   2   1

Printed in the United States of America

     ∞ TM The paper used in this publication meets the minimum requiren
            American National Standard for Information Sciences—Perman
            Paper for Printed Library Materials, ANSI Z39.48–1984.

Contents

Acknowledgments

The production of any book indebts the author to innumerable persons both directly and indirectly. There is a sense in which one feels the necessity to thank anyone who ever offered a word of encouragement, served as a sounding board for ideas, provided a shoulder to cry on, and so on. This, however, can become an impossible task.

Nevertheless, there are those persons whose contributions, both personal and professional, cannot go without recognition: Sheila Briggs, in whose office the idea for this book was born, and who nurtured its development to maturity; Lois Banner, who provided invaluable guidance and critique for the historical sections; and Ron Hock, whose rigorous reading of several drafts helped me to focus my ideas and to ensure that what I said was what I meant. To all three I wish to express my gratitude, not only for their knowledge and expertise, but for the gracious and supportive manner in which it was given.

In addition I want to thank my fellow members of D.A.G.: Mark Kowalewski, Lois Lorentzen, Carlos Piar, Bob Pierson, Fredi Spiegel, Bron Taylor, and David Tripp. Without their unflagging friendship and support I never could have finished this work. Most of all I thank them for keeping me accountable. I am also indebted to Kelli Gilbert, whose careful editing helped smooth out the rough spots and made this a more readable book.

I also must thank my parents, William and Shirley Say, who provided enough love, faith, and encouragement to carry each of their six children securely into adulthood. I particularly want to express my gratitude to my mother who undertook the painstaking task of proofreading the final manuscript. And, of course, my acknowledgment of familial support must include Gino Virgili who provided me the emotional and intellectual space in which to work.

Finally, I dedicate this to the memory of my foremothers, Bertha E. Say and Margaret A. Holder. Throughout my life they provided an example of strong, capable, independent women, and are an inspiration to me still.

Introduction

In the preface to her book, *Diving Deep and Surfacing,* Carol Christ reflected on her own experience as a graduate student in a Religious Studies program. During her studies she became aware of an increasing sense of incongruence between her own spiritual experiences and the theological language that was available for the articulation of those experiences.

> Gradually I began to wonder whether I had a different perspective on theology because I was a woman. . . . If theology were written from a male perspective and my perspective was female, that might explain why my professors and student colleagues . . . often failed to understand my perspective on theological issues.[1]

When I read this passage I recognized it as the expression not only of my own experience, but also that of many other women that I have met during my years as a student of religion. Whenever I discussed Christ's book with other women we all tended to respond in a similar way: We identified with her experience and felt a sense of relief in knowing that we were not alone.

Christ's book resonated with the perceptions of other women who have entered into what has been, until recently, an almost exclusively male discipline. What has become increasingly clear to women is that since women's experience of the world has been so different from that of men, and since men have dominated theology, it would be almost impossible for traditional theologies to provide an adequate framework for the expression of this experience.

The task with which women theologians are faced is the creation of

1

new theologies that are congruent with women's experience. The question is, how is one to go about doing this? "The expression of women's spiritual quest is integrally related to the telling of women's stories. If women's stories are not told, the depth of women's souls will not be known."[2] This was the starting point of Christ's book, and it is my starting point as well.

Most theological language that is available is based on men's stories: stories told about men's lives and interpreted from a distinctly masculine perspective. In such stories women, by and large, are marginal characters. When they occasionally do figure in a more central role, the meaning of their actions is explained from a male viewpoint. Before women can begin to ask questions about the meaning of their experience, they must understand what this experience has been, and this requires the telling of their own stories, in their own voice.

The assertion that stories are an important basis for theological argument is a theme that is not articulated only by women. Male scholarship is also engaging in new reflections on the use of narrative as a ground for theological and moral debate. This is reflected in the developing interest in "narrative theology" by Michael Goldberg, Stanley Hauerwas, and Alasdair MacIntyre, to name only a few. These theorists begin with the premise that stories provide the context for understanding the meaning and purpose of our existence and therefore are, of themselves, a type of moral or theological argument.

When I first began to read the work of some narrative theorists and theologians, I thought perhaps that here, at last, was an approach to theology that would be amenable to women's lives. There is, after all, much in common between the perspective of narrative theologians and the concerns expressed by feminist theologians. The foundational premise of the significance of stories, the experiential nature of theology as reflected in the authority of a life lived, and the efficacy of stories as a means of empowerment (for both storyteller and audience) were themes articulated by both groups.

And yet, despite the apparent similarities, I had a nagging sense that at a fundamental level they were at odds. My first insight as to what the source of this disagreement might be came when I was reading Phyllis Trible's *Texts of Terror*. Feminists have argued that women must tell our stories in our own voice which, as Carol Gilligan made clear, is a voice different from that of men. Narrative theologians have also emphasized the importance of understanding a story in the context of the community it serves. For most of history, however, women's stories have been told through the voice of others, and women have only recently begun to reclaim and retell these stories from the perspective of their own experience. Thus, Trible explains the purpose of her recounting of four "texts of terror."

> It interprets stories of outrage on behalf of their female victims in order to recover a neglected history, to remember a past that the present embodies, and to pray that these terrors shall not come to pass again. In telling sad stories, a feminist hermeneutic seeks to redeem the time.[3]

The problem with this is, of course, that it is the retelling of women's lives—women who could not speak for themselves, so we must speak on their behalf—of their suffering, their strength, their defeats, and their victories. We speak to fill the chasm of silence with the sound of women's voices.

I began to wonder, however, about the stories we do have in women's original voice. When did that voice begin to make itself heard? How has our hearing it impacted our lives? How was women's experience of telling their story different from that of men? If, as narrative theologians claim, our stories are antecedent to our theologies, then the story of women telling their stories must inform the theologies we derive from the narrative.

The emergence of women as storytellers was a phenomenon of the nineteenth century. This is not to say that women did not write and tell the stories of their lives before this time, but it was the establishment of the woman novelist that brought women's heretofore relatively private voice (as expressed in letters, diaries, conversation, etc.) into the world of literature and hence the public realm.

Although Christ used the word narrative in a broad sense, I am going to restrict this study to a much narrower field and discuss narrative expression as it is found in the novel only.[4] The reason for this is, in part, because the novel is the modern narrative form. As I will discuss in chapter three, some theorists have argued that modern conceptions of self and society are as much a creation of, as they are reflected in, the novel. If this is so, then novelistic narrative is intrinsically related to the modern era. Therefore, any discussion of women's contemporary use of narrative must account for the novel.

In addition to this symbiotic relationship between the modern self and the novel, it was through this genre that women were first to gain a public voice. Virginia Woolf was perhaps the first to note the significance of the emergence of women novelists in the late eighteenth century, suggesting that this was of more historical importance than the Crusades or the Wars of the Roses.[5] In the following century women came to dominate the literary world as the major creators and consumers of novels. As a new literary genre developed, women were central to its formation and continued to employ it as a primary means of expression. For these reasons, it is important to understand not only the way women's stories can form a basis for theology, but also the ways in which women have used a specific narrative form, the modern novel, as a vehicle for moral expression and argument.

As I examined the development of women as novelists, the source of the disparity between male narrative and feminist theologians began to clarify itself. It was not a disagreement about the function of narrative as a ground for theology. Rather, it was reflected in the purpose that narrative was seen to serve. Narrative theologians look to narrative to restore a lost vision of community, which plagues the modern world. While feminist theologians have emphasized the importance of women's stories as a means to facilitate female bonding, in the broader arena of patriarchal society women have told their stories as a way of identifying the deceit of the myth of community. As women increasingly made their voices heard, it became clear that a woman's experience of discontinuity with the world in which she lived was not an isolated event: The personal was political. The community that men seek to restore was that which marginalized women's lives and which women cannot embrace.

The emergence of the woman novelist began the process of identifying the experience of women's lives within a society dominated by men. Women's reality was seen through the eyes of women, not interpreted by those who stood outside it.

It could be argued that, although women first gained a public voice through the novel, they are no longer confined to this form of discourse, and therefore the novel is less important in women's lives. However, if the premise of narrative theology is correct—that it is through our stories we come to create and understand ourselves—then the story of the emergence of women as novelists makes a claim on contemporary women, and on the development of a feminist methodology of narrative theology. This claim is grounded in the belief that the act of women telling their stories poses a fundamental challenge to patriarchal reality. It is, as Christ has made clear, a claim to the power of naming that reality; what men have called community, women have named oppression.

> The simple act of telling a woman's story from a woman's point of view is a revolutionary act: it never has been done before. . . . Women writers

who name the gap between men's stories about women and women's own perceptions of self and world are engaged in creating a new literary tradition. . . .[6]

To understand the significance of the novelist as a teller of women's stories, it is necessary to examine the development of women's public voice. Therefore, I have chosen to restrict my study primarily to the nineteenth century. In addition to reasons already given, there are other considerations for this focus. To invert Dickens's famous opening to *A Tale of Two Cities,* it was the worst of times, it was the best of times. On the one hand, at the beginning of this period, due to the emergent middle-class construction of separate spheres, woman's position was exceedingly circumscribed. However, it was during this same century that the battle for women's rights began to gain momentum, and great strides forward were made, culminating with the vote in the early twentieth century. I will argue that both these apparently antithetical factors were directly related to the development of the novel, and that the ideal of the domestic woman, which limited woman's activities, would also, by enabling the expression of her public moral voice, serve as an agent of her liberation.

Although the concept of separate spheres is one that has been written about extensively, it is important enough to my argument to warrant a brief examination of what this entailed for women in the nineteenth century. The first chapter, therefore, will look at what was required by the "cult of domesticity" and how this impacted on the actual lives of women, particularly in the assessment of women's moral superiority and the need to provide for the "redundant woman." These two factors, while a result of the concept of separate spheres, would pave the way for the emergence of women into the public realm.

Part of the struggle for the betterment of women's situation included the fight for women's education. The arguments surrounding this battle can provide insight not only about the nineteenth-century attitudes toward women, but also into why certain disciplines were more accessible to women while others remained resistant. These insights, in turn, can help to clarify why and how women have employed narrative as a forum for moral argument.

The second chapter will therefore focus on the claims of nineteenth-century women to be granted a liberal education comparable to that of their fathers and brothers. I have chosen to restrict this to the struggle for women's education as it was carried on in England, especially the battle for university degrees. The reason for this is strictly practical.

Although England was the center of a large colonial empire, and therefore manifested a diversity of ethnic and cultural histories within its populace, this diversity was not reflected within the academic system. The great universities sought to produce graduates who conformed to essentially the same mold; that of the proper English gentleman. The university experience helped to create an essential homogeneity and to minimize the difference between the young men who participated in it. Because of this it is easier to make general observations about the cultural values and attitudes that the university system helped both to create and maintain.

Since the university was seen as the training ground for young men preparing to enter the public realm it, too, became part of this sphere. For this reason it was not considered an appropriate place for women, and their attempts to earn degrees met with virulent opposition. It was not until the late nineteenth century that women began to gain admittance to the universities, and even this did not change the firmly entrenched attitude that this was not a proper endeavor for women. Women who entered into academic pursuit were viewed with suspicion as "unwomanly" women.

The nineteenth century was a period in which the universities were undergoing other changes as well that would affect both their curriculum and structure, most notably, perhaps, the trend toward professionalism. These changes impacted on the direction that women's education would take, and as I will argue, contributed to the continuation of women's use of the novel as a primary means of moral and theological expression.

The third chapter will examine the novel as a genre and consider whether or not there is something intrinsic in its structure that made it an especially effective means of expression for women. Thirty years ago, when Ian Watt wrote *The Rise of the Novel,* he suggested that the novel was a response to demands of middle-class sensibilities. However, more recent studies have argued that the development of the novel was part of the process of epistemological and social changes that began in the seventeenth century. As such it provided a vehicle through which an emerging middle class would create and define itself. The novel, therefore, was not so much a response to an existent middle class as it was one of the primary tools for its construction.

One of the defining characteristics of middle-class England was the concept of separate spheres and the resultant elevation of the domestic woman as a locus of moral authority. The novel began to define and establish this during the eighteenth century, and within a century it was firmly established. Although early nineteenth-century novels tended to celebrate this, by the end of that century women were using the novel to challenge the ideal.

The novel also participated in the establishment of the paradigm of the self-determining individual, which was central to middle-class identity. This, too, was a significant development for the lives of women since it provided a context within which a woman's experience could serve as a ground for moral argument.

The novel acted as a mediator for all these changes. It provided a medium for moral debate about the meaning and purpose of individual lives, and because the novel was the literature of choice for the middle class, it brought these arguments before the general public. The centrality of women as authors of novels enabled the expression of women's voices in debates that had heretofore been the province of men.

The concept of separate spheres, the internal changes undergone by the universities, and the role of the novel as a forum for public moral argument were all influential in the transition of women out of the private sector. By the end of the nineteenth century they were concerned less with the issue of the appropriateness of their new position than they were with utilizing narrative to redefine the public sphere.

There were many women who used the novel in this manner, however, in chapter four I will focus on one in particular who benefited from all these combined factors, Dorothy L. Sayers. Sayers began her career as a writer as the creator of the Lord Peter Wimsey detective stories. After ten years of writing novels, she then tackled theology, and her theological reflections were firmly based on her experience as an author. Her understanding of creative work as divine imaging provides one further suggestion for examining the significance of women as storytellers. Sayers argued that it is in the process of creation that human beings reflect God. If this is the case, then the woman novelist also makes a theological statement. The right to create had been a primarily male prerogative. Therefore, when women began to write they claimed for themselves the ability to reflect the divine image in the same manner as men.

In this assertion, Sayers provides a warrant for understanding women's experience as a theological ground. Although theology has always been grounded in human experience (primarily the experience of white, male intellectuals), this remained a largely unexamined component of theological discourse. It was not until the modern era, with its emphasis on the authority of individual experience, that the experiential nature of theological presuppositions began to be challenged. It is still the case that women must continually justify their assertion that women's experience is as valid a ground for understanding the sacred as the experience of men. Sayers's work provides one method of claiming this authority.

As an illustration of the way in which Sayers employed her novels as a means for making both moral and theological arguments, I will examine her final detective novel, *Gaudy Night,* and her treatment therein of the meaning of human work and relationships.

Finally, in the last chapter I will address the question of the relationship of women's narratives to narrative theology. Narrative theologians assume that stories can provide a foundation for the restoration of a sense of community that has been lost in modern society. It is this assumption that is problematic.

Stories provide the basis for the creation of a tradition, and it is one's understanding of her place in that tradition that enables action toward a future. The tradition of Western culture, based on the stories of men's lives, is primarily a masculine tradition. This is not to say that women have not been included in it, but their inclusion has been as receivers, not creators. The expression of women's experience is a relatively recent phenomenon, and although women have begun the task, they are far from being able to identify and claim a tradition. Therefore, while masculine narrative theologies seek to find new possibilities for commonality, women's stories are still in the process of defining the nature of their incongruence, and their theologies must, necessarily, serve a different purpose.

Some final remarks about the way I have approached this subject are required. While I will deal extensively with the historical development of women's narrative voice, this is not a history. I am not a historian, and am therefore wary of wading into too-deep water. This is, rather, a theoretical reconstruction of the nineteenth century, which is largely dependent on the research of qualified historians. I proceeded on the premise that all societies have their "ideal types" that function as the operative paradigm for evaluating individual lives, even when the reality of those lives falls short of the ideal. The woman of the 1990s, for example, labors under the burden of the "superwoman" who can successfully manage career, home, family, and personal relationships. This woman assaults us at every hand: She is the president of a megacorporation; she lives in a home that would win the Good Housekeeping seal of approval; she has two highly intelligent children and a husband who all idolize and adore her; she is active in civic affairs;

and her clothes, hair, and make-up are always flawless. I have yet to meet this woman, but it took me a long time to realize that, if she does exist, she is probably in therapy.

In the same way, the ideal of the nineteenth century was that of the "Angel in the House." While I have tried to account for the fact that this was a model achieved, in reality, by very few women, it is clear that it was the paradigm against which women were measured. It also served as the basis for proscriptions against women as they sought to move beyond the boundaries it established. The emergence of woman's public voice must, therefore, be understood as rebellion against a normative standard of acceptable female behavior.

In addition, although I will consider the claims of narrative theology, the reader should not anticipate that I have developed an alternative, feminist methodology of narrative theology. What I have attempted is a critique of narrative theology from a feminist perspective. What I have sought to clarify is the nature of the differences between the vision represented by narrative theology and the revisioning that is inherent in women's stories. In so doing I hope to have suggested some issues that a feminist methodology must address—but that is another project.

I end this brief introduction, then, as I began it, with a quote from Carol Christ.

> When one woman puts her experiences into words, another woman who has kept silent, afraid of what others will think, can find validation. . . . Their act creates new possibilities of being and living for themselves and for all women. With the creation of a new language, the possibility that women will forget what they know is lessened.[7]

NOTES

1. Carol P. Christ, *Diving Deep and Surfacing: Women Writers on Spiritual Quest* (Boston: Beacon Press, 1980), xi.

2. Christ, *Diving Deep,* 1.

3. Phyllis Trible, *Texts of Terror: Literary-Feminist Readings of Biblical Narratives* (Philadelphia: Fortress Press, 1984), 3.

4. Christ, *Diving Deep,* 1. Christ includes as narrative "all articulations of experience that have a narrative element, including fiction, poetry, song, autobiography, biography, and talking with friends."

5. Virginia Woolf, *A Room of One's Own* (San Diego: Harcourt Brace Jovanovich, Publishers, 1929), 68.

6. Christ, *Diving Deep,* 7.

7. Christ, *Diving Deep,* 23.

1

The Early Struggle for Female Education: Changing Paradigms

Much has been written about the changes that occurred in Western culture as the result of the Industrial Revolution. This was, of course, true of Great Britain, as well as other countries. Two changes brought about by industrialization that were especially significant in the lives of English women were the rise of a middle class and the removal of many traditional forms of female labor from the home to the factory. In fact, these two developments cannot be isolated from one another. It is not my intention to catalogue these changes, but simply to remind the reader of how they affected the position of women in society.

The pre-industrial world was characterized by a relative lack of separation between home and work.[1] By and large, home and work were bound together. England was predominantly agricultural, and the basic means of livelihood was the family farm. A family produced what was needed for its own survival, or traded for goods produced at the local market. For those who lived in urban settings, such as artisans and shopkeepers, enterprise was still a family business, and all family members participated.

In such a setting, a woman's contribution to the family had economic value. The ideal for womanhood was that of the "perfect wife" who was an active participant in the family's well-being.[2] Not only did she bear children to increase the family's labor pool, but she also was responsible for the production of food and clothing, educating her children, and helping in the daily management of the family enterprise.

This is not to say that women enjoyed social or political equality with men; society was patriarchal. However, the contributions of a wife had economic worth. The Industrial Revolution changed this. Manufacturing was taken out of the home and placed in the factory. Trade for goods was replaced by cash for goods as the primary means of exchange, and since men were the primary wage-earners, it was men's labor that came to have value, and men's sphere (the public world of enterprise) that gained in importance while the private world of the home suffered loss of value.[3]

This is, of course, an oversimplification of the state of affairs. The fact is that among the less-well-off classes, women (and children) also went to work in factories. However, since women were paid less than men, and since the wage was the measure of a person's worth, women's work was still devalued.[4]

This leads to the second development of industrialization that affected women: the rising middle class. The expansion of factories meant not only the shift of labor for working-class men, but also the opening up of new fields of endeavor as business bureaucracies expanded. There were a growing number of professional men—managers, salesmen, accountants, and so on—and these men (and their families) came to constitute the middle class.

Although I will discuss the influence of this class in more depth in chapter three, at this point I simply want to note that the middle class came to have an increasingly determinative influence on the cultural and social expectations of England, so that by the nineteenth century the prevailing standard was that of the middle class. The conception of the role and place of women in society that I will be discussing in this chapter is a specifically middle-class ideal. However, since the middle class came to set the tone for Victorian society, it was an ideal that affected both the aristocratic and the working classes as well. In spite of the fact that even many middle-class families could not live up to the expectations, it nevertheless set the standard.[5]

One observer has noted that the Victorian middle-class outlook was characterized by both self-confidence and anxiety due to the rapid social and economic changes that were occurring.[6] The self-confidence was occasioned by increased prosperity enjoyed by the growing middle class. Upward mobility was a greater possibility than ever before. One's son could be educated with the aristocracy; one's daughter (provided with an enticing dowry) might marry above her class. However, the same progress that occasioned this optimism also produced anxiety; traditional values seemed in flux.

In response the Victorians sought to mediate these tensions by defining certain institutions in a way that resolved them.[7] As a result, the home was elevated in its position as the primary refuge from the hostile world of enterprise. The home became the guardian of Christian virtues; the public world of enterprise was the place of capitalist values. The development of the concept of separate spheres was a middle-class construction, and it affected women in many ways.

A woman's labor was not valued so much for its contribution to the family's economic stability as it was for its moral and emotional—its interpersonal—contributions. The concept of separate spheres of endeavor for men and women established a dualism, and masculinity and femininity became defined as opposites. What it meant to be a man was, above all, not to be a woman. The character traits thought necessary to succeed in the public world were identified as masculine. What it meant to be feminine, then, was to be the opposite of this.

If masculinity was to be concerned with the public world of business, then femininity was to be concerned with the private world of emotions and relationships. A new ideal developed that served to both promote and defend the notion that a woman's proper place was in the home, the private sphere. This has been identified as the "ideal of true womanhood" or the "cult of domesticity."

These two appellations provide insight into the focus of this ideal. In the first place, women's domestic chores and the efficient running of her household were elevated to new heights. A woman's self-expression was to be achieved through the maintenance of clean floors, snowy linens, and a well-stocked pantry. In addition to this, however, was the idea that the true woman would find complete satisfaction in the domestic sphere. Her highest calling was to create an atmosphere in which the external factors of cleanliness and order reflected an internal harmony of the persons who lived within a home. The true woman was able to manage both these tasks.

Not only were women responsible for the tasks required in the smooth running of a household, they also came to be seen as holding the keys to the maintenance of interpersonal peace and tranquility. Woman's sphere increasingly came to be seen as that of the emotions, relationships, and personal morality. A woman's highest calling was to the instillation of lofty moral values in her children. In fact, as Nancy Armstrong has argued, the creation of the middle-class domestic woman gave women a moral authority superior to that of men.[8]

However, this definition of masculine and feminine as opposites also affected women in another way. As I have noted, the Victorian era was a period of redefinition of both womanhood and manhood. It was the Victorians who created the image of the successful man as "self-sufficient, aggressive, competitive, a good 'provider' for his sheltered family."[9] Again, while this was a particularly middle-class ideal, it affected conceptions of manhood throughout society.[10] Womanhood was understood to be in contrast to this: an inversion of the male image. Therefore, if men were self-sufficient women were dependent; if men were aggressive women were passive; if men were competitive women were idle.

This idea of women as idle may seem incongruous in light of the standard of the cult of domesticity. However, for middle-class Victorians it came to be increasingly idealized. There were two primary indicators of social status in the Victorian period, and the Victorian woman was key in both. The first of these was material wealth. It was a mark of a man's success if his wife and daughters did not have to do the actual housework themselves. His wife might be in charge of overseeing the running of the household, but she should not have to actually labor. A good provider would provide servants for this. The second indicator was "the manifestation of certain personal and cultural attributes," or gentility.[11] The husband might be responsible for earning the money, but the style of family life achieved was the responsibility of the wife. Again, this quality of gentility was tied to an ideal that removed women from practical work. It became a status symbol for middle-class women to be able to live in luxury and idleness.

> The backwash of the late eighteenth-century Romanticism had produced an exaggerated respect for refinement and sensibility, so that the further removed from toil of any kind, the more delicate and empty-headed, the more of a lady was a woman held to be.[12]

As a result, the ideal of the "perfect wife," which was characteristic prior to and at the beginning of the nineteenth century, had by mid-century given way to the ideal of the "perfect lady."

I should note, once again, that this ideal is one that was probably achieved, in reality, by very few Victorian women (a point I will return to later), but it was the reigning paradigm of the day. The strength of this image of the perfect lady can be seen in the fact that women's advice magazines of the day often deplored the idleness and frivolity of the contemporary woman, even though it is unlikely that most of the readers of these magazines lived a lifestyle that approached the standard of the paradigm.[13]

The middle-class wife and mother who had not achieved this standard of idleness could hope that her daughter would marry well and achieve it. This standard also became the goal of working-class women and men. The factory girl dreamed of the day when a man would rescue her from her drudgery and enthrone her in a home of her own. The laborer worked toward the day when his wife and children could leave the factory or mill. For both the middle and lower classes the ultimate mark of success was a lifestyle that enforced the idleness, passivity, and dependency of women.

THE CHARACTERISTICS OF THE "PERFECT LADY"

Although I have mentioned briefly the expectations of the concept of separate spheres, I want to examine them in greater depth, because they had a profound influence on the discussions regarding female education. The ideal for women was characterized, first and foremost, by a woman's absolute dependency and total devotion to a man (preferably her husband, but in his absence, her father or brother would do). The woman a man wished to marry was the domestic angel and perfect lady, and to become this meant the renunciation of all of one's own desires and aspirations.

> I believe this . . . is a perfect ideal of an English wife and mother, kind, considerate, self-sacrificing, and sensible, so pure-hearted as to be . . . so unselfishly attached to the man she loves, as to be willing to give up her own wishes and feelings for his sake.[14]

It is easy to see why, from a male perspective, this might be considered the perfect wife and mother. However, a woman penned the following advice: "The love of a woman appears to have been created solely to minister; that of man, to be ministered unto." She goes on to say that any sacrifice a wife may make for her husband's comfort is well worth the effort and is more likely to elicit his good will in response than if his wife had "been all day busily employed in writing a treatise on morals for his especial benefit. . . . It is unquestionably the inalienable right of all men . . . to be treated with deference, and made much of in their own houses." She concludes by saying that even if a woman should have the misfortune to marry a bad husband, she still owes him this deference because she voluntarily entered into the relationship and placed herself in a position of subordination.[15]

Of course, we might ask whether such a relationship could really be considered voluntary in a society where, outside of marriage, women had very few options, and these were fairly dismal.

John Ruskin, one of the chief champions of separate spheres, perhaps sums up best the reasoning behind this concept and the necessity for women's dependence on men.

> The man's power is active, progressive, defensive. He is eminently the doer, the creator, the discoverer, the defender. His intellect is for speculation and invention. . . . But the woman's power is not for rule, not for battle,—and her intellect is not for invention or creation, but for sweet ordering, arrangement, and decision. . . . Her great function is Praise. . . .[16]

This dependence on men imposed obligations on the wife. In return for his support and protection, she was to create a refuge for him; an escape from the hard reality of the public world.

> This is the true nature of home—it is a place of Peace. . . . And wherever a true wife comes, this home is always round her . . . to fulfill this, she must . . . be incapable of error. . . . She must be enduringly, incorruptibly good; instinctively, infallibly wise—wise, not for self-development, but for self-renunciation. . . .[17]

The reason for her dependence, then, brings us to the second important feature of the concept of separate spheres. Women were dependent on men because they were opposite from men. If man's nature suited him for the public world (and this was taken as a given) then, by definition, woman's nature was suited for the private realm. If, as Ruskin asserts, she must be "incorruptibly good," then she could not possibly function in the public realm, because this was a corrupted and corruptible environment. The man had to protect her from it, not only for her own good but also for his own well-being.

> For most males luxuriating in dominance, a woman deserting her assigned sphere not only became something of a freak, a man-woman; she also raised uncomfortable questions about man's own role, a role defined not in isolation, but in an uneasy contest with the other sex.[18]

It cannot be stressed overmuch that the Victorians believed that this difference in natures was intrinsic, was divinely ordained. For this reason, to cross the boundaries would upset the balance of society. Man needed the shelter of a loving wife and home as much as woman needed, it was believed, the protection of her husband. God, in his wisdom, had given men and women different natures that complemented each other. This idea was so profoundly held that even men who supported some aspects of women's fight for legal rights never questioned the assumptions that lay behind separate spheres. A Baptist preacher who supported women's suffrage nevertheless maintained that

[Woman's] mental and bodily capacity point both in the same direction, and mark her out for the same sphere. The body which unfits her for the rough competition and jostling which belongs to public life, is not matched to a mind which requires to move in that public sphere. . . .[19]

Woman's uncorrupted nature was necessary to balance the regrettably corrupted—but unavoidably so—nature of man. The delicate balance of good over evil in the world was maintained by the influence of women who were protected from the public realm. Women were thought to be morally superior to men. They were pure, compassionate, loving, and giving; all the things that a man's necessary involvement with the world kept him from being. Therefore, if women did not remain in their proper sphere this balance would be upset, and women would be responsible.

There is not a war in the world, no, nor an injustice, but you women are answerable for it; not in that you have provoked, but in that you have not hindered . . . there is no suffering, no injustice, no misery in the earth, but the guilt of it lies with you—Men can bear the sight of it, but you should not be able to bear it.[20]

This paradox of woman's nature—that she is morally superior to man and at the same time lacking qualities that are necessary for moral action—was an appearance most women would find hard to maintain. On the one hand she was required to be ignorant of all male concerns, for only by such ignorance could her moral purity be preserved, yet she was required to devote herself to the moral improvement of men. One cannot help but suspect that such ignorance was oftentimes feigned.

This quality of ignorance is the third requirement for the maintenance of separate spheres, because for the Victorians ignorance equaled innocence. Young women were sheltered as much as possible from the realities of life because this idea of the innocent woman was expected and desired by men who would be potential husbands.[21]

Knowledge of the "real world" would spoil a woman and would tarnish her purity. "Ignorance and innocence were confounded . . . women who sought knowledge were held to be unnatural."[22]

Coventry Patmore's popular "The Angel in the House" reflects this ideal of innocence. The image of the Angel required a level of childishness; a woman who was never quite an adult.[23] In order to maintain this, it was believed that the girl should be kept morally untested, under the watchful eye of her mother, in her father's home, until she was handed over to her husband. It was an image of "blank virtue" as opposed to tried virtue, which was expected of men.[24]

One modern critic of the Victorian Age has observed that for "Respectable Victorians . . . 'innocence' or 'pure mindedness' or 'inherent purity' was an exalted state of feminine consciousness, a state of unique deficiency or mindlessness in their daughters of . . . the knowledge of good and evil."[25] It was believed that women retained a remnant of the innocence of Paradise, and this led them to protect their chastity (highly valued by the Victorians). Once this innocence had been lost, a girl's chastity became vulnerable. Therefore, parents sought to preserve their daughter's innocence by protecting her from reality.[26]

> Moral responsibility presupposed freedom of choices as well as the knowledge of moral alternatives. Victorian culture and the genteel family withheld the knowledge from their daughters and their responsibility for choosing . . . innocence absolved daughters from the exercise of responsibility.[27]

The goal, of course, for every young woman was marriage, and toward this goal she was trained from her youth. Unmarried daughters represented financial burdens for their fathers and suffered social ostracism in an age where a woman's value was measured by her role as wife and mother.

> Parents who are anxious "to marry off" their daughters, know that a woman of independent spirit might hesitate to enter into a state in which "her being and legal existence are suspended"; and therefore they educate them to be dependent . . . till they end by becoming mere drawing room ornaments, scarcely so useful as a French clock or a firescreen, when young, and when old . . . entrapping young men of fortune into marrying their daughters, as they themselves were married before them.[28]

EDUCATING THE "PERFECT LADY"

The state of female education in the mid-nineteenth century reflects this ultimate aim for Victorian womanhood. Although it was accepted by middle-class families that a son should receive an education that would fit him for competition in the public realm, since their daughters would not be engaged in the same competition they did not need a similar education. The purpose of their education was different from the purpose of their brothers'. "For their sisters, achievement was not a central goal."[29]

For both boys and girls religious training was very important, although more so in the early and mid-Victorian period. Children were taught the fundamentals of the Christian faith from their early years. However, the emphasis of their instruction was different for boys and girls. For girls, a greater emphasis was placed on the duty of self-sacrifice and the other self-effacing Christian virtues.[30]

In addition, while it was considered appropriate, even necessary, that a boy be educated away from home (if the family could afford it), the opposite was deemed appropriate for girls. Since a girl's proper sphere of activity was the home her education should again take place at home, under the watchful eyes and close supervision of her mother. Although many guides to the raising of daughters suggested that they be sent off to expensive finishing schools, most middle-class families could not afford to do so; the money that was available for education was spent on the sons.[31] For the same reason most families could not afford to hire governesses. If a girl was lucky enough to have a brother for whom a tutor had been engaged, she might be able to share in some of his education. But, for the most part, education came from their mothers. Since their mothers had been educated in a similar manner, the quality of girls' education suffered. For example, girls were usually uninstructed in classical languages and higher mathematics (both deemed crucial to a young man) since these subjects were not necessary for domestic competence.[32]

Because most girls were educated at home, their education also suffered from a lack of standardization. Even if they were sent away to a school for "young ladies" there were no standards of educational excellence to be met. Some girls received a good education, but many recieved an education that was inadequate or nonexistent. Emphasis was placed on rote learning, which made education tedious, "but it could never produce a serious mastery of any skill or branch of knowledge. In fact, its shallowness was intentional, and considered appropriate to women's limited powers and subservient condition."[33]

Much of the education that a young woman or girl received was what has been called "ornamental education" and reflected the notion that women were to be ornaments in the home of their father or husband.

"[T]he real end and use of all such [ornamental] attainments . . . [is] to supply her hours of leisure with innocent and amusing occupations . . . and contribute to preserve the mind in a state of placid cheerfulness."[34]

Because of the perceived difference in the nature of men and women, it was believed that girls did not need, nor could they accommodate, the rigorous demands of their brothers' education. It was suggested that girls "want more an education of the heart and feelings, and especially of firm, fixed, moral principles . . . with a sure groundwork of religion and obedience. The profoundly educated women rarely make good wives or mothers."[35]

Since it was expected that all girls would grow up to become wives and mothers, girls were not educated to get jobs; the goals of their education had no practical aim. "[T]he purpose of education for girls was to create perfect young ladies out of them and [their] education . . . was generally moulded by this aim."[36] Toward this aim, girls were advised that their attitude toward their studies should be neither "frivolous" nor "over serious."[37] When girls were dealing with the masculine, strong subjects (e.g., mathematics) they ought only to learn enough to make them good listeners for men, but never for the purpose of displaying their knowledge. Girls were "advised that they should never be interested in learning for its own sake."[38] A women's magazine in the 1840s gave the following suggestion as to what should comprise a young woman's education: "Languages, Music, Dancing, Painting and the light accomplishments; a sound religious education will supply most other deficiencies."[39] Since a woman's goal was marriage, preferably to a wealthy man, little else was deemed necessary.

Anything that might make a young woman unmarketable as a wife was to be strenuously avoided. Martha Vicinus has noted that a girl's education was designed to bring out her " 'natural' submission to authority and innate maternal instincts." She was trained to have no opinions because this would make her less attractive to a future husband. She was to be a blank page on which her husband could write his will.[40]

Girls' education was "to make them pleasant and useful companions to men, and responsible mothers to their children."[41] Of course, one has to wonder how a girl was supposed to develop into the paragon of virtue that was the ideal of Victorian womanhood if her education and training focused on frivolity and remained entrenched in shallowness.

Women of the day wondered about the same thing. Writing in 1843, one woman observed that

> the education of girls . . . does not . . . tend to expand and develop their minds, but to cramp and confine them. . . . The consequence . . . is, that the majority of girls are subdued into mere automatons. . . . All the good they do is towards others, their own minds all the while lying barren and unfruitful.[42]

More than twenty years later, a supporter and pioneer of improved education for women bemoaned the fact that the education of girls had not altered much in the intervening time.

> The education of girls has too often, been made showy, rather than real and useful—accomplishments have been the main thing, because these would enable a girl to shine and attract, while those branches of study especially calculated to form the judgment, to cultivate the understanding and to discipline the character . . . have been neglected; and thus . . . the great ends of education have too often been lost sight of.[43]

If, however, one accepts the premise that knowledge corrupts innocence, and innocence is necessary to female virtue, then these arguments, as reasonable as they sound, carry little weight. Again, a quote from John Ruskin supports this prevailing opinion. Regarding the education of women Ruskin maintained that

> All such knowledge should be given her as may enable her to understand, and even to aid, the work of men: and yet it should be given, not as knowledge—not as if it were, or could be, for her an object to know; but only to feel, and to judge.[44]

Writing thirty years later, a critic observed that Ruskin's hostility to the question of the emancipation of women was so deep that his criticism of such movements "never condescends to reason."[45] Nevertheless, Ruskin's "Of Queen's Gardens," published in 1865, was widely popular, and the sentiments he expressed therein were generally supported. "She is to be taught somewhat to understand the nothingness of the proportion which that little world in which she lives and loves, bears to the world in which God lives and loves. . . ."[46]

Finally, if all these arguments did not convince the young girl that education was not meant for her, there was one more appeal that could be made; education was dangerous to her health. Puberty and the onset of menstruation were thought to be a particularly vulnerable time for the Victorian girl, and this was an opinion held by both the medical professionals and the lay person. Anything—travel, activity, emotional stress—could disrupt the cycle of nature. Since the purpose of womanhood was motherhood, this could be disastrous. Especially dangerous during this time was excessive study.[47]

> Let it be considered that the period of the real educational strain will commence about the time when, by the development of the sexual system . . . an extraordinary expenditure of vital energy is made. . . . The energy of a human body being a definite and not inexhaustible quantity, can it bear, without injury, an excessive mental drain as well as the natural physical drain which is so great at that time?[48]

Education, then, was a danger not only to the feminine ideal of the Victorians, but also to the health of Victorian womanhood. "In short, the best safeguard against abnormal menstruation and the ills that might accompany it, was rigorous conformity to the Victorian ideal of femininity."[49]

THE IDEAL CONFRONTS REALITY

The problem with the Victorian ideal of femininity, supported by the concept of separate spheres, was that it was difficult to maintain in the face of reality. In the first place, most families did not have the income to support wives and daughters in the ornamental idleness that gentility mandated. The middle-class housewife was much more likely to be "an active agent in the family, not a pampered woman of leisure, yet her functions could easily outstrip her means."[50] Although few women fit the ideal, the ideal remained nevertheless, and women who did not fit were perceived as "lacking."[51] And, of course, this was the middle-class ideal; for the working woman it was an impossibility by which she was nevertheless measured.[52]

Patricia Branca has argued that most middle-class Victorian women did not fit the picture of the "perfect lady." They had neither the time nor the money for a leisure life, and were as much concerned with and involved in the process of modernization as were their male counterparts. They were enthusiastic about modern labor-saving appliances for the home and were interested in modern theories about personal health and contraception.[53] However, there nevertheless remained

> an uncertainty among many of these women about the new ways, even as they largely persisted in them. . . . Victorian society, in terms of its

official culture, was very demanding of its women. It expected them to be perfect ladies, perfect wives, and perfect mothers. . . . For women, the adverse public culture could not only cause feelings of guilt about new patterns of behavior but could inhibit a consciousness of the significance of their behavior.[54]

Even if a family managed to maintain the standard demanded by the ideal, the question remained whether this could indeed create the qualities of moral excellence that were required. It was much more likely that idleness would lead to boredom, and boredom to triviality, frivolity, and small-mindedness. "No pure and noble minded woman can . . . submit passively to, a vicious and dissipated—or even to a good and virtuous tyrant—without having her own mind greatly deteriorated."[55]

In an effort to allay this, women were counseled to find some good work to do, but this work could not be recompensed. "The most popular alternative to vacuity for middle classes was charity."[56] Charity work was deemed appropriate for women because it was in accord with their nurturing natures. But even here, the scope of *real* work that a lady might properly undertake was narrow, and so women tended to dabble in charity, but without any real commitment.[57]

Over and above all this, of course, is the reality that out of financial necessity women of the middle class often found it necessary to work. A reduction in her father's circumstances, or his death, could force the young woman from her place of shelter into the harsh world of reality, for which she was little prepared. If this were to happen, she lost her status as a lady. Marion Kirkland Reid, writing in the mid-nineteenth century, asked what was to become of such women. Should they be condemned for their behavior, which was considered so abhorrent? Should they be "exterminated?"

Or if we charitably allow them to cover their sins under the strong plea of necessity, what are we to think of that state of society which absolutely forces thousands of unfortunates to contradict their own nature—not by enlightening or enlarging their sphere—but by thrusting them entirely out of it?[58]

Although some maintained that this situation was an unavoidable evil, she asked whether "it [is] fair to continue institutions which in their turn perpetuate those absurd prejudices which make it next to a certain loss of caste for any woman to attempt earning an honest and independent livelihood for herself?"[59]

Over and above the problem of those women who might be called upon to help support themselves and their families until rescued by marriage or, once married, to help their husbands, was the whole problem of "redundant women." In a society that defined a woman's value by her role as wife and mother, those women who never fulfilled this role were deemed superfluous. "The majority of middle-class women were vaguely assumed to be wives and mothers, for whom home-making was the sole job compatible with their desires and suited to their qualifications."[60] However, the 1851 census revealed that in actuality there were 876,920 "redundant" women.[61] The question was, what was to be done with these surplus women?

Many people proposed answers as to how to resolve the problem of the redundant woman; some were sensible, some ludicrous. One writer suggested that the solution was to have these women emigrate to the British colonies where there was a great deficiency of women. "We must restore by an emigration of women that natural proportion between the sexes in the old country and in the new ones, which was disturbed by an emigration of men, and . . . which has wrought so much mischief in both lands. . . ."[62]

Unmarried women were seen as so unnatural that they were a source of humor for the Victorian mind. Since a middle-aged woman could no longer be considered innocent and ignorant, it was thought funny that she should want marriage, or that a man would want her. "All social forces combined to leave the spinster emotionally and financially bankrupt."[63]

There were other suggestions as to how to resolve this problem, such as the following sound advice: "The plan then which I advocate for providing for superfluous women is that of allowing them to engage freely in all occupations suited to their strength . . . thus converting them into useful members of society."[64]

The problem was, what kind of work were these women suited for? Raised in middle-class homes, with middle-class notions of propriety, they could not possibly go to work in factories as working-class girls did. In fact, the very idea of work for remuneration was so antithetical to Victorian ideals of femininity that any job tainted her delicacy and lowered her status.

The image of the lady as a creature of leisure, closed within a private circle of family and friends and completely supported by father or husband, was reinforced by the ban on paid employment—a ban so strong that many who wrote for publication, even though writing at home, did so under pseudonyms, or signed their work simply "By a Lady."[65]

For those women who had not the talent to earn a living by the pen, there was only one other socially permissible occupation; that of governess.

The position of governess was not thought as dangerous for a young woman because after all, she still remained in a home setting. In addition, she would be surrounded by persons of the proper class, since only the relatively well-to-do could afford governesses. Finally, since she herself had been raised to be a lady, it was assumed that she would be well-equipped to impart this knowledge to those under her charge.

The reality of the situation was quite dismal. In the first place, there were more women in need of jobs as governesses than there were positions available. "Too often the financial disasters of parents involved the unwilling departure of daughters. . . . Since there is never a scarcity of misfortune, more governesses existed than posts for them to fill."[66]

Additionally, the idea that she would be received as a member of the same class and be afforded a place in the family was also misguided. "She was neither a guest nor a member of the family with whom she worked; by birth a lady, she was economically in the position of a servant."[67]

The worst problem, however, was that for the most part she was appallingly bad at her job. Her own education had not equipped her to teach anyone anything. "A girl forced to take up work as a governess not only did not know how to teach but did not know what to teach."[68]

It was a growing realization of the plight of the unmarried woman that became the springboard for educational reform for women.[69] The problem of redundant women was not going to disappear. If these women were going to have any useful place in society, then they would have to be equipped for it. However, the answer was not simply to establish training schools for governesses, because most middle-class families did not plan on their daughters needing to work; they planned for marriage. Women only took jobs as governesses out of dire necessity, and by the time necessity struck, it was too late for training.[70] The solution was to improve the overall education of middle-class girls.

The early rationale behind the movement for improved education, then, was not fundamentally at odds with prevailing Victorian sensibilities. If not all women could be married, it was much better than they be suited, by virtue of a proper education, for a position in keeping with their upbringing. In addition, supporters were quick to point out that a better education would only serve to make a woman a better wife and mother.

> . . . [E]very woman is, or ought to be, a teacher, or at least she should be able to teach. If the casualties of life never force her from her home . . . May she not become a mother? . . . We may therefore safely assert, that no woman is really able to perform the duties which devolve upon her, be her station what it may, unless she has herself been well educated. . . .[71]

In the year 1847, in London, a series of lectures was organized by proponents of female education. These came to be known as the Lectures for Ladies.[72] By 1848 these had developed into Queen's College, London, which was established to educate girls over the age of twelve. "This institution actually undertook to teach 'all branches of female knowledge'—an apparently stupendous undertaking limited by the qualifying adjective at a time when knowledge was regarded not as a human necessity, but as a male prerogative."[73] A year later, in 1849, a second, similar institution was also opened in London: Bedford College. Both of these institutions envisioned their primary goal to be that of training young women for careers as governesses or school teachers. But in addition to the many who came for this reason they also attracted daughters of well-to-do families who wanted an education for its own sake.[74]

> In opposition to the deadening nineteenth-century view of women as helpless though adorable creatures of inferior mental and physical ability, a small group . . . believed that women shared a common humanity with men and should be allowed to realise their intellectual potential . . . [and others] questioned the contemporary treatment of women. . . .[75]

When these two institutions opened, few people envisioned the direction in which they would lead. But the demand for a liberal education for their daughters, equal to that of their sons, led middle-class parents to expect a higher level of academic accomplishment from their daughter's teachers than had heretofore been required. This need for teachers who were better trained and more thoroughly educated set the tone for the struggle for women's admittance into the great universities of England.

NOTES

1. Janet Horowitz Murray, *Strong-Minded Women and Other Lost Voices from Nineteenth-Century England* (New York: Pantheon Books, 1982), 4;

Margaret L. Anderson, *Thinking About Women: Sociological and Feminist Perspectives* (New York: MacMillan Publishing Co., 1983), 103–4.

2. Martha Vicinus, "Introduction," in *Suffer and Be Still: Women in the Victorian Age* ed. Martha Vicinus (Bloomington: Indiana University Press, 1972), ix.

3. Anderson, *Thinking About Women*, 105.

4. Anderson, *Thinking About Women*, 105.

5. See Patricia Branca, *Silent Sisterhood: Middle-Class Women in the Victorian Home* (Pittsburgh: Carnegie-Mellon University Press, 1975). Branca argues that in actuality most middle-class housewives of this period did not live lifestyles that measured up to the image of genteel leisure prescribed by the middle-class ideal. Her work is based on the examination of women's magazines, particularly from the second half of the nineteenth century.

6. Deborah Gorham, *The Victorian Girl and the Feminine Ideal* (Bloomington: Indiana University Press, 1982), 3.

7. Gorham, *Victorian Girl*, 4.

8. See Nancy Armstrong, *Desire and Domestic Fiction: A Political History of the Novel* (New York: Oxford University Press, 1987).

9. Murray, *Strong-Minded Women*, 9.

10. Peter N. Stearns, "The Emergence of the Middle-Class Man," in Peter N. Stearns, *Be A Man!* (New York: Holmes & Meier Publishers, Inc., 1979), 79–112.

11. Gorham, *Victorian Girl*, 8.

12. Katherine Moore, *Victorian Wives* (New York: St. Martin's Press, Inc., 1974), xiv.

13. Branca, *Silent Sisterhood*, 35.

14. William Acton, *The Functions and Disorders of the Reproductive Organs, in Childhood, Adult Age, and Advanced Life, Considered in the Physiological, Social, and Moral Relations* (1875), cited in Murray, *Strong-Minded Women*, 129.

15. Sarah Stickney Ellis, "The Wives of England" (1843), cited in *Women, the Family, and Freedom: The Debate in Documents*, vol. 1, 1750–1880, ed. Susan Groag Bell and Karen M. Offen (Stanford, Calif.: Stanford University Press, 1983), 193–94.

16. John Ruskin, "Of Queen's Gardens," in *Essays and Letters Selected from the Writings of John Ruskin*, ed. Mrs. Louis G. Hufford (Boston: Ginn & Company, 1894), 81–82.

17. Ruskin, "Of Queen's Gardens," 83.

18. Peter Gay, *The Bourgeois Experience: Victoria to Freud*, vol. 1, *Education of the Senses* (New York and Oxford: Oxford University Press, 1984), 169.

19. William Landels, *Woman: Her Position and Power* (1870), cited in Murray, *Strong-Minded Women*, 214.

20. Ruskin, "Of Queen's Gardens," 99.

21. Moore, *Victorian Wives,* xvi.

22. Rita McWilliams-Tullberg, *Women at Cambridge* (London: Victor Gollancz Ltd., 1975), 20.

23. Gorham, *Victorian Girl,* 6.

24. Vicinus, *Suffer and Be Still,* ix.

25. Peter T. Cominos, "Innocent Femina Sensualis in Unconscious Conflict," in *Suffer and Be Still: Women in the Victorian Age,* ed. Martha Vicinus (Bloomington: Indiana University Press, 1972), 157.

26. Cominos, "Innocent Femina Sensualis," 157.

27. Cominos, "Innocent Femina Sensualis," 160.

28. Caroline Francis Cornwallis, "Capabilities and Disabilities of Women," review article in the *Westminster Review* 67, no. 131 (January 1857), cited in Bell and Offen, eds., *Women, the Family,* 311.

29. Gorham, *Victorian Girl,* 24.

30. Gorham, *Victorian Girl,* 19.

31. Branca, *Silent Sisterhood,* 45; Gorham, *Victorian Girl,* 20.

32. Gorham, *Victorian Girl,* 22.

33. Murray, *Strong-Minded Women,* 197.

34. Thomas Gisborne, *Duties of the Female Sex* (1797), cited in Murray, *Strong-Minded Women,* 198.

35. Sarah Sewell, *Women and the Times We Live In* (1868), cited in Murray, *Strong-Minded Women,* 213.

36. Barbara Rees, *The Victorian Lady* (London: Gordon & Crenonese, 1977), 17.

37. Gorham, *Victorian Girl,* 103.

38. Gorham, *Victorian Girl,* 105.

39. Rees, *Victorian Lady,* 21.

40. Vicinus, *Suffer and Be Still,* x.

41. Gorham, *Victorian Girl,* 102.

42. Mrs. Hugo Reid, *A Plea for Women* (1843), cited in Murray, *Strong-Minded Women,* 212.

43. Dorothea Beale, "The Ladies College at Chetenham," *Transactions of the National Association for the Promotion of Social Science* (1865), cited in Patricia Hollis, *Women in Public 1850–1900: Documents of the Victorian Women's Movement* (London: George Allen & Unwin, 1979), 137.

44. Ruskin, "Of Queen's Gardens," 85–86.

45. J. A. Hobson, *John Ruskin: Social Reformer* (Boston: Dana Estes & Company, 1898), 285.

46. Ruskin, "Of Queen's Gardens," 87.

47. Gorham, *Victorian Girl,* 85–87.

48. Dr. Henry Maudsley, "Sex in Mind and in Education," *Fortnightly Review* (April 1874), cited in Murray, *Strong-Minded Women,* 221.

49. Gorham, *Victorian Girl,* 89.

50. Branca, *Silent Sisterhood,* 22.

51. Vicinus, *Suffer and Be Still*, xi. Gorham, *Victorian Girl*, 10–11.

52. Moore, *Victorian Wives*, xix. Vicinus, *Suffer and Be Still*, xiii.

53. Branca, *Silent Sisterhood*, 149–52.

54. Ibid., 152.

55. Marion Kirkland Reid [Mrs. Hugo Reid], "Woman: Her Education and Influence" (1857), originally published as *A Plea for Woman* (1843), cited in Bell and Offen, eds., *Women, the Family*, 198.

56. Vicinus, *Suffer and Be Still*, xi.

57. Vicinus, *Suffer and Be Still*, xi.

58. Reid, "Woman: Her Education and Influence," 198.

59. Reid, "Woman: Her Education and Influence," 198.

60. Vera Brittain, *The Women at Oxford: A Fragment of History* (London: George G. Harrap & Co. Ltd., 1960), 25.

61. Brittain, *Women at Oxford*, 25.

62. W. R. Greg, "Why Are Women Redundant?", *National Review* (April 1862), cited in Hollis, *Women in Public*, 37.

63. Vicinus, *Suffer and Be Sill*, xii. Nina Auerbach also notes that the old maid was the object of derision in Victorian society. Nina Auerbach, "Old Maids and the Wish for Wings," in Nina Auerbach, *Woman and the Demon: The Life of a Victorian Myth* (Cambridge, Mass.: Harvard University Press, 1982), 109–49.

64. Jessie Boucherett, "How to Provide for Superfluous Women," (1869), cited in Hollis, *Women in Public*, 41.

65. M. Jeanne Peterson, "The Victorian Governess: Status Incongruence in Family and Society," in *Suffer and Be Still: Women in the Victorian Age*, ed. Martha Vicinus (Bloomington: Indiana University Press, 1972), 6.

66. Brittain, *Women at Oxford*, 26.

67. McWilliams-Tullberg, *Women at Cambridge*, 22.

68. McWilliams-Tullberg, *Women at Cambridge*, 22.

69. McWilliams-Tullberg, *Women at Cambridge*, 20.

70. McWilliams-Tullberg, *Women at Cambridge*, 22.

71. Mary Atkinson Maurice, *Mothers and Governesses* (1847), cited in Bell and Offen, eds., *Women, the Family*, 175.

72. Brittain, *Women at Oxford*, 27.

73. Brittain, *Women at Oxford*, 28.

74. Brittain, *Women at Oxford*, 28.

75. McWilliams-Tullberg, *Women at Cambridge*, 23.

2

University Education: Undermining an Ideal

The struggle that ensued in the second half of the nineteenth century, and on into the twentieth, for the granting of university degrees to women is a fascinating story. It reveals much about the strength, determination, and intelligence of the women who refused to be turned away from the citadels of male privilege. It is not, however, my intent to chronicle these events; others have done a thorough job of this.[1] What I am interested in are the debates that this struggle engendered, and the way in which these debates reflect certain attitudes about the role of women in society. In addition, these attitudes provide insight into how and why narrative was to become a vehicle of particular attraction for women.

In order to narrow the focus of this examination, I have chosen to concentrate on the debates that revolved around the admission of women to Oxford and Cambridge. On the one hand this is a purely pragmatic decision, because it makes this project eminently more manageable; but there are also other, less instrumental reasons for my decision.

In the first place, it has been argued that Oxford and Cambridge set the standard not only for university education in Great Britain, but also for cultural values and norms. The standards of academic excellence established by these two great universities affected the curriculum at schools where young boys were educated. Boys were educated so that they would be able to pass the public examinations offered by the universities. As the movement for the reform of girls' education expanded, they followed this lead.[2]

In addition to being the measure of academic pursuit, these two institutions had a profound effect on the cultural identity of Britain. Since they were considered to be the epitome of intellectual achievement, young men who received their education at Oxford and Cambridge were able to take leading positions in society.

> Since their foundation the Universities of Oxford and Cambridge have exerted a unique influence on the course of English history, more especially in the realms of culture, politics and religion. From an early date the universities were the places at which the future leading members of the established classes received their final education; nor was the Universities' position in this respect challenged significantly . . . until the middle of the twentieth century.[3]

Because of the unique position that Oxford and Cambridge occupied in the hearts and minds of their countrymen (and women), the debates that took place regarding the admittance of women gained wide publicity. "The domination of public life by Oxford and Cambridge men ensured that the affairs of the old universities were of national concern and among the central domestic issues of the day, at least before the First World War."[4]

Oxford and Cambridge are also interesting because they were both so thoroughly strongholds of male privilege and power. Until the relaxation of the celibacy rules in the late nineteenth century, they were almost exclusively male enclaves.[5] For this reason, the prospect of the presence of women, particularly young, unmarried women, was cause for a great deal of alarm.

For all the foregoing reasons it was around the issue of granting degrees to women at Oxford and Cambridge that the most heated debates centered. Other British universities granted degrees to women long before these two institutions did so. For example, in 1896 Oxford was still debating the question of whether or not women were constitutionally able to withstand the rigors of academic life. "At this date London University had been giving degrees to women for seventeen years, and the Scottish universities for three."[6] Oxford determined to deny degrees to women that year, and Cambridge followed suit: ". . . anti-feminism gains so firm a hold that Cambridge University postponed degrees for women until 1947."[7] Oxford preceded them in the granting of degrees by about twenty-five years. The firmly entrenched opposition to women in both universities made for fierce arguments that reveal much about the participants' attitudes toward women and education.

Finally, Oxford and Cambridge are particularly interesting for this study because of their close affiliation with the Church of England. Vera Brittain made clear that in 1850 Oxford was a "man-created citadel of static theological and classical tradition. . . ."[8] The same can be said for Cambridge. The government of both universities was controlled by members of the Church. In virtually all colleges at both Oxford and Cambridge "the statutes were religious in tone and intention, asserting that the object of the foundation was to train men in the Christian faith. . . ."[9] Because it was viewed as a training ground for future clerics, the opposition to women can be understood not only as resistance to women encroaching on a masculine intellectual monopoly, but also to women who dared broach the walls of that other sacred male domain, theology. "At all times [Oxford and Cambridge] occupied a central position in English religious life . . . because . . . they were the leading centres of theological exposition and enquiry and the chief training ground for ministers of the church."[10]

Because of all these factors the struggles of women at Cambridge and Oxford are an excellent reflection of the intellectual and cultural ideologies that surrounded the debates regarding women and education in general, and women and theology in specific. "It is arguable that throughout the history of the Church in England the Universities of Oxford and Cambridge have exerted a determining influence, helping to shape and direct the developments which have governed its life."[11]

In the preceding chapter I examined the cultural assumptions about woman's nature and role, and the corresponding development of the social construct of separate spheres. Although, as we have seen, this concept did not represent the reality of many women's lives, it nevertheless remained the paradigmatic ideal of middle-class England. As a result, when women began to demand admittance into the universities, this ideal provided the framework for resistance. Although it should be obvious what sort of objections were raised against the admittance of women, I want to briefly clarify the nature of these.

THE INCOMPATIBILITY OF WOMEN'S NATURE AND THE UNIVERSITY

A quote from Annie Rogers's chronicle of the quest for degrees at Oxford helps to establish the two main objections to women's presence. ". . . [A]n eminent scholar . . . [believed] that the students would be under the domination of priests, and . . . an eminent theologian . . .

that they would all be atheists."[12] On the one hand, the intellectuals seemed to think women so feeble-minded and weak-willed as to have no mind of their own. Theologians, representing the other side of the argument, believed that a woman wanting a university education was so out of God's order that the only ones who would seek it were those who had cast aside all belief.

The idea of women receiving an education equal to that of men cut to the very heart of Victorian sensibilities and threatened the exclusive preserve of male power. Men perceived, quite rightly, that once women gained admittance to university education the walls that surrounded their carefully guarded territory would begin to crumble. As a result they waged a mighty defense. "Patronizing, often slandering women, men tried to keep not only what they had long possessed but also what they had recently acquired."[13]

In the face of this opposition women and their male supporters worked slowly but steadily toward their goal. The latter half of the nineteenth century was a period of increasing awareness of the social inequities regarding women, and this consciousness served the campaign for education well.

> The movement to admit women to universities, both old and new, owed much to a developing realization of the need to instruct gifted women and train their judgment, so that they might discover how to use and not abuse power; to abandon the evasive weapons of weakness, and learn to rely on the direct use of strength.[14]

What, then, were the claims brought against women? In the first place, it would be necessary for young women to live away from home. This had always been considered a crucial part of a young man's education. It was understood that in addition to the intellectual training he would receive, he would also experience, by virtue of university life itself, preparation for his emergence into "real life." The university imparted not only knowledge but also certain attributes of character deemed necessary for all young men. He would learn independence, self-confidence, the value of competition, as well as discretion in judgment; all necessary attributes if he were to be successful in public life. However, as we have seen, these very qualities that were considered invaluable to a man were thought to be antithetical to the Victorian ideal of femininity. ". . . [C]ollegiate life was desirable for men because it fostered independence and boldness . . . the life of most women would be quite the reverse . . . their very virtue was dependence."[15]

A woman's proper sphere was the home; this was her place of expression and protection. How could she be guarded if taken out of this sphere? In addition, since the universities were almost exclusively male, the idea of women going to live in their midst offended ideas of propriety.[16] At a time when it was considered improper for a young woman to be alone with a man, the idea of them living in close proximity without the watchful eyes of parents observing every movement was outrageous. This fear of impropriety continued to plague women in the university throughout their struggle. For example, women were required to attend all lectures in the company of a chaperon; this practice continued at Oxford until 1920.[17]

In addition to questions of propriety, there were also medical objections to overcome. It was generally held that although a young man's nature was suited to the rigors of academic life, a young woman would crumble under the stress.

> . . . [T]here is just this difference between the making of a girl's character and a boy's—you may chisel a boy into shape, as you would a rock, or hammer him into it, if he be of a better kind, as you would a piece of bronze. But you cannot hammer a girl into anything. She grows as a flower does. . . .[18]

Not only would university life affect a young woman's emotional stability, it also would affect her physical health. "The competition that . . . a young woman would unavoidably encounter should she go on to pursue higher education, was held to be physically damaging. . . ."[19] By the 1870s some doctors, especially the new breed of woman physicians, were opposing this idea. In 1874, Dr. Elizabeth Garrett Anderson, Britain's first licensed woman physician, wrote in rebuttal to Dr. Henry Maudsley.[20] She pointed out that women's education would not be so strenuous if they did not have to fight for it every step of the way. Second, she noted that a large part of the stress in university life was due to competition for fellowships, and since the fellowships were not open to women, they were relieved of this burden of competition. Most importantly, however, she said that education was far less damaging than the imposed boredom and idleness that was the usual fate of young women, leading them into premature marriages and general unhappiness.[21] For the most part, as was to be expected, the ideas of Dr. Anderson and others who agreed with her "had limited impact on society as a whole."[22]

This idea that women and men are, by nature, different both physically and emotionally, was also paralleled by the belief in different mental capacities: Women were generally considered inferior. The argument about women's intellectual capabilities plagued the reform movement from the beginning. The first step in raising the standard of female education was to gain admittance to the public examinations held by Cambridge and Oxford, and from the very first there was discussion as to whether or not girls should take the same exams as boys. On the one hand, the objection to identical exams had a practical foundation: The examinations given to boys contained Latin and Greek, and higher mathematics, subjects in which girls traditionally had no training. Many argued that it would be unfair to test girls in subjects for which they would be at an obvious disadvantage. But others felt that on general principles the boys' examinations were too demanding and would place undue stress on females.[23]

However, Emily Davies, one of the early pioneers for equal education, recognized that if special "women's examinations" were offered they would continually fall under the criticism of not measuring up to male standards. If female students were to gain recognition it must be by the same standards that males were required to meet.[24]

In 1865 Cambridge agreed to extend its Local Examinations to girls for a three-year trial period. In 1867 this arrangement was made permanent. Oxford did not open its exams until 1879. The opening of the examinations to girls helped to raise the standard of female education generally; there was now a goal towards which to work. "The preparation of girls for public examinations became commonplace and the curriculum generally followed that of the best boys' schools."[25] Much to the chagrin of those who opposed them, the young women who took these exams generally did as well as their male counterparts.

Based on the assumptions regarding the physical, emotional, and intellectual inferiority of women, we find another cause for opposition to university education. Since it was assumed that this subordinate position was natural, indeed, that it was divinely ordained, the implication was that any young woman who sought higher education was some kind of freak. The fear of the "unwomanly woman" was rampant.

> The one thing men do not like is the man-woman, and they will never believe the College, or University, woman is not of that type. . . . Such a cultivation as will make a really good wife, sister, or daughter, to educated men, is the thing to be aimed at. . . . No one of the slightest experience can contemplate without very great alarm the effect of indiscriminately applying the system of men to women. . . .[26]

Ridicule was thrown at women for being unwomanly; it was claimed that they wanted rights because no man would have them. "The male citadel was under siege, and there was no point pretending that the besiegers were either gentle or pretty."[27] If woman's true calling was home, husband, and motherhood, the inference was that women who did not make these things their first priority were not true women. "At the end of the century, girls were still advised, even by those most committed to their education, that they should perceive that education as a preparation for 'woman's mission': for femininity and domesticity."[28]

A sermon preached at Oxford in 1884 sums up the masculine attitudes toward the unwomanly woman. The speaker attacked the university woman as "a proposed reversal of the law of Nature which is also the law of God governing women. . . ." He concluded that "inferior to us God made you, and inferior to the end of time you will remain. But you are none the worse off for that."[29] The position of women was not only the cultural norm, it was rooted in divine ordinance. Indeed, Annie Rogers called this sermon a "combination of sentiment and theology."[30]

This fear of the "man-woman" reflects, finally, one last objection to university women. Since women and men were defined in opposition to one another, and since the masculine sphere was maintained by the existence of the feminine, men feared the intrusion of women into their world. "The real strength of the opposition lay, not in any alleged care for the education or health of women, but in a dislike and fear of their presence in the University."[31] Competition with women in the male domain and, worse still, feminine success in that competition, threatened the very bedrock of masculine identity. If being a man meant being the opposite of women, and yet women were able to perform successfully in hitherto male-only arenas, it might necessitate a redefinition of masculinity. This fear led even so "enlightened" and educated a man as the sociologist Herbert Spencer, who believed in the lifting of some legal restrictions from women, nevertheless to write "any extensive change in the education of women, made with the view of fitting them for business and professions, would be mischievous."[32] This idea, that the intrusion of women was perceived as a threat to masculinity, is one that I will return to in more depth at a later point.

In order to better understand the resistance to women at Oxford and Cambridge, it is necessary to look beyond the debates that focused solely on this issue, for this was not the only reform movement taking place at the universities. The latter nineteenth century was a time of general upheaval at both institutions as age-old traditions sought to accommodate a modern world. Again, I will not attempt to catalogue all the events of this period since others have done so.[33] However, certain changes that took place had a direct bearing on the struggle of women.

STRUCTURAL AND CURRICULAR CHANGES IN THE UNIVERSITIES

Although Oxford and Cambridge had a long-standing and close affiliation with the Church of England, during this period the strong ties with the Church begin to weaken. In the early nineteenth century (and before) the Oxford don was a clergyman, not a university teacher. Holy orders were a condition of fellowship. Fellowships were held until a clerical living opened up, at which point the fellow would leave to become a parson.[34] The university was not a career; it was merely a step on the way to a career. Its purpose, by and large, was to train men for the ministry, and for this reason the university "advanced knowledge, but more as a by-product of its activity in education than as an end."[35] In addition to preparing clergy, the universities also functioned to educate the upper classes who would become the leaders of society. To this end their goal was to "educate in virtue as well as knowledge."[36]

Prior to mid-century, subscription to the Thirty-nine Articles of the Church was required before any young man could take his degree. However, although the acts of 1854 and 1856 opened the lower degrees to persons of any religion, or no religion at all,[37] it was not until 1871 that university officials were no longer required to take religious tests, and 1882 when clerical fellowships were no longer the majority.[38] The move away from Church domination was slow, and subject to much debate. It was due in part to a general trend toward secularization in the overall society, and in part toward a new focus on education within the universities themselves. "Their religious importance was waning, in part because the Universities were themselves becoming more and more secular institutions and in part because religion itself was ceasing to play a fundamental part in the life of the community."[39]

This gradual withdrawal from Church governance was occasioned by and affected other reform movements within the universities. First of all it was part of a movement to make education a profession.[40] Throughout the nineteenth century the great majority of university dons were "gentlemen" awaiting a clerical living. Their fellowships supported them until a living became available. However, there were usually more fellows than livings, and the wait for a position could be long. The question was, how could these men earn a livelihood and still retain their gentlemen's status? This problem led to the movement for the professionalization of academia.[41] The last thirty years of the century "saw the universities . . . as institutions, made neutral in religion . . . and as places of academic enquiry, far more detached in their study of religion."[42]

It should be noted that the trend toward professionalization was not exclusive to the universities. The second half of the nineteenth century saw similar movements within the realm of enterprise. In fact, the increasing emphasis on the concept of the businessman as a professional could not but affect the universities, because it occasioned an increased demand for higher education. Middle-class men were, more and more, working in state and business bureaucracies, and academic criteria increasingly became a factor in hiring decisions.[43]

This move toward professionalization brought about changes in university curriculum and structure. There was, on the one hand, an increasing demand on the part of the tutors for recognition of their teaching function. They claimed that the primary goal of the universities ought to be that of education. They argued that unless teaching was made a profession, and rewarded accordingly, it would be impossible to attract men of high caliber to the role of teacher.[44]

There was also, at this time, an increasing emphasis from others on the obligation of the university to advance knowledge and there was a push for increased funding for research. Both of these movements served to undermine the influence of the Church.

These new directions for the universities also brought changes in curriculum. For example, there was an increasing demand that Greek and Latin be dropped as mandatory for examinations. The argument was that these were only necessary for those going into holy orders, and that modern languages might better suit the pursuance of science. There was also a growing interest in new subjects such as English Literature and Language.[45] The University Commissions of 1850 and 1877 opened the door for new disciplines to be introduced and made religious skepticism in the name of intellectual inquiry respectable. The influence of the Church diminished even further.[46]

The demand for professionalism also led to a relaxation of the celibacy rules. Because clerical fellowships were intended to be only a stepping stone to a ministerial position, they had never been designed to support a wife or family. Indeed, it was thought that one way to prevent a young man from wanting to retain his fellowship overlong was to make celibacy a condition for holding it. However, if teaching was to be a career, then the celibacy statute could not be retained. The 1877 commission opened the door for the relaxation of this demand also.[47]

The increasing move toward professionalization and secularization of the universities could not help but affect the place of theology in their curriculums. Before this period of study of religion among undergraduates had a dual purpose. On the one hand it was to indoctrinate all young men in the fundamentals of Church teaching, while at the same time preparing those who would go on to holy orders. With the new push toward research and academic inquiry came a demand for "scientific theology."[48] The study of theology was gradually removed from its domination by the Church and was opened to both non-Anglicans and non-believers.[49]

Another factor that would affect the decreasing role of the Church was the First World War. After the war inflation caused financial difficulties for both universities and they found themselves needing to appeal to the State for funding. The Royal Commission of 1922 granted financial assistance to both universities, but at the expense of a degree of autonomy.[50] The students who returned to the universities after the war were also of a different type. There was an increased skepticism and it was noted that "the general characteristic of the present generation is aimlessness and its besetting fault incapacity or unwillingness to think coherently on any subject, least of all on religion."[51]

THE THREAT TO MANHOOD

When one takes into account all the changes that the universities in general, and the Church factions in particular, were undergoing, it is not surprising that many viewed the incursion of women as especially insidious. Education and religion had been exclusive male preserves. It was bad enough to be faced with a loss of control and autonomy to other male powers (i.e., the State), but the thought of having to relinquish these even further to women caused these institutions to tremble on their very foundations. The reaction against women in education was, after all, only part of the larger reaction against the overall militancy for women's rights in the latter nineteenth century. To many men it appeared that their dominance was being challenged on every front, and they reacted accordingly. When one's sexual identity is defined by the maintenance of separate spheres, the breakdown of this division becomes a genuine threat. "The sense that manhood was in danger deepened as the campaign for women's rights picked up momentum."[52]

The nineteenth century was a period in which definitions of masculinity were undergoing redefinition on many fronts, resulting in a general unease about conceptions of manhood, especially among middle-class men. It should not be surprising that men reacted to this by denigrating women.[53]

Peter Gay has argued that this perceived threat to manhood was counteracted by the nineteenth-century idea of women's moral purity and lack of sexual appetite. He calls this, in the language of Freud, a "reaction formation," a psychological defense. These type of defenses are "maneuvers that convert impermissible or horrifying thoughts into their opposite: sadism into pacifism, fear of effeminacy into ostentatious toughness. . . . Many men . . . experienced feminism in all its forms as nothing less than a threat of castration."[54]

Gay points out that this fear of women can be found continuously throughout history and cites example after example of images of women destroying men (e.g., Medusa, Eve, Delilah, Cleopatra, etc.). But the nineteenth century, according to Gay, raised this obsession to new heights. In its portrayal of the ideal woman as near-angelic, the contrasting paradigm came to be seen as near-demonic.[55]

> The nineteenth century reduced this female to a type, . . . the dangerous woman came to constitute one of the leading themes in the literary and artistic imagination of the century.[56]

Nina Auerbach has argued persuasively that the conception of the demonic woman is, in fact, the "flip side" of woman as angel. The conception of women as angels went against traditional Christian theology in which angels had been masculine. Although within the social realm the Angel in the House might have been restricted, this ideal nevertheless provided an image that was potent with the possibility of power. The images of women as demons were the logical extension of this possibility gone wrong. A woman was more likely to be a demon "because by definition, woman is an angel."[57]

As women's demands for the vote, for education, and for legal rights increased, so did male hostility. As women continued to push in the boundaries of male territory, the accusations of "unwomanly!" grew louder. "[N]o century depicted women as vampire, as castrator, as killer so consistently, so programmatically, and so nakedly as the nineteenth. . . ."[58] According to Auerbach, "In the Victorian imagination the danger of woman's special powers produced the foot-binding of her officially approved image."[59]

Gay does point out that this thesis is reductionistic and incomplete since not all male anti-feminists were this slanderous, not all men were anti-feminists, and not all anti-feminists were male. However, it does provide insight into the resistance to women in the universities in general, and in theology in particular.

The arguments against admitting women to degrees reflects this fear of emasculation. I have already noted Annie Rogers's observation that the opposition to women at Oxford was based on a "fear of their presence in the University." In 1896, Professor Percy Gardner, Chair of Classical Archeology at Oxford argued that granting women degrees would " 'thoroughly assimilate' the education of the sexes and lead to a 'softening of moral fibre.' "[60] Cambridge experienced similar fears. The rivalry between the two universities was strong, and both were afraid that if they admitted women it "would result in an exodus of the best men to 'the other place.' "[61]

Both institutions shared the perception that the presence of women within their halls was dangerous. After all, the maintenance of all-male universities was founded on the premise that women, by their very nature, could not compete in the masculine realm. Therefore, if women were to participate, the universities would have to lessen their standards to accommodate the lesser capabilities of women, and this could not be permitted. Of course, there was one other possibility: that the male assumptions about women's nature were wrong and, therefore, also their assumptions about men. This was not a pleasant thought. Just as the Victorians abhorred an "unwomanly woman," so, too, they despised an "unmanly man." Since their notions of manhood rested on the concept of separate spheres, any man who welcomed women into his privileged enclave became questionable.

The admittance of women also threatened emasculation because it would mean competition between the sexes. Since it was generally held to be unmanly to take advantage of the weaker sex, competition meant one of two things. Either women were not intrinsically weaker, or men were not fully men. And of course, if women competed for degrees, might they not also compete for jobs, moving even further into men's domain? ". . . [T]he question of competition was no longer just one of offending manly pride. There was a real fear that women would compete with men for jobs."[62] This fear, which existed in 1897 at Cambridge, was still evident in 1921 when the major concern was "the ever-present fear of competition which lay behind so many of the curious excuses which were given for not admitting women to degrees."[63]

Finally, the university men feared that if they admitted women to degrees, women might actually gain control of the government of the institution. Once an individual was granted a degree, he was permitted to vote on university matters. It was believed that if women were able to vote on university issues, they would interfere in men's affairs. ". . . [T]he education of the middle and upper-class young male was held to be an exclusively masculine affair . . . it was feared [women] might attempt to meddle in men's education, altering it, in some unspecified way, to [women's] own advantage."[64]

If women were perceived as a threat to the universities in general, this perception was intensified when it came to the study of theology. Taking Gay's thesis that the reaction against women was the result of a fear of emasculation, this might have been felt particularly by men in the Church.

The idea of theology as an exclusively masculine domain has always seemed a little strange to me in view of the Victorian concept of woman's nature, for the Victorians believed that women had an intrinsic affinity for piety and religion. Their whole concept of the moral superiority of women rested on the belief that women (by virtue of their absence from the public realm) were less corrupted than men and retained a greater degree of the original innocence. Women were encouraged to develop their religious nature, and indeed, religion was thought to be a most appropriate activity for women. Women were, for example, significant contributors to religion in the writing of hymns and other devotional literature.[65] It would seem that above all other disciplines theology would be the one considered "safest" for women's minds to tackle.

However, women were barred from participation in theological discourse. "Religious commitment and expression was, after all, an approved outlet for female assertiveness—within limits."[66] The limits imposed seem not to have been on account of the subject matter but rather the methodology. Affective piety is not forbidden; theology is. Theology, dependent on intellectualism, implies authority and knowledge, both of which were forbidden to women.

> . . . [U]ntil the twentieth century women occupied virtually no positions of leadership or responsibility in the official life of the Church at any

> level. . . . They were excluded both from spiritual leadership and from
> secular management. Women's sphere in the late Victorian Church was
> decidedly subordinate, limited and controlled everywhere by the author-
> ity of men.[67]

Outright injunctions against women involving themselves in theology
are not easy to find, but the lack of them seems to come more from the
common assumption of the impropriety of it than from a lack of
disapproval. It was taken for granted that women should not do
theology. After all, theology was for those in holy orders, and since
women could not be ordained, there was no reason for them to study
or write theology. Additionally, given the masculine assessment of
women's intellectual capabilities, the task of theology must have
seemed beyond the limits of a woman's mind.

However, John Ruskin did make an impassioned plea that women
stay away from this discipline.

> There *is* one dangerous science for women—one which they must indeed
> beware how they profanely touch—that of theology. Strange, and miser-
> ably strange, that while they are modest enough to doubt their powers,
> and pause at the threshold of sciences where every step is demonstrable
> and sure, they will plunge headlong, and without one thought of incom-
> petency, into that science in which the greatest men have trembled, and
> the wisest erred. Strange . . . [that they] . . . think to recommend
> themselves to their Master, by scrambling up the steps of the judgment
> throne, to divide it with Him.[68]

The same critic who accused Ruskin of "never condescending to
reason" in his reaction against women, nevertheless thinks that there
is a "subtlety of wisdom . . . in his express prohibition of theology, as
fraught with peculiar danger to women. . . ."[69]

Several years later, when Ruskin was delivering his Inaugural Lectures for Oxford, he "astonished the company with a rant against . . .
women who brood on the sufferings of Christ instead of alleviating the
sufferings of men."[70]

Knowing something about the background against which this tirade
is set is helpful in understanding Ruskin's reasoning. In his middle age
years Ruskin became enamored (one might say obsessed) with an
eleven-year-old girl named Rose La Touche. She was to him the ideal
of Victorian femininity; the "Angel in the House." She was obedient,
dependent, docile, adoring, submissive—all the requisite qualities. Of
course, the fact that she was only a child helped. When she reached
the age that he could decently propose to her he did so, and to his

extreme surprise she rejected him. Ruskin could not reconcile himself to the change in Rose from docile child to willful woman. He perceived, quite rightly, that her rejection was due to her religious convictions.[71]

Rose felt that Ruskin had fallen away from the truth of Christianity. As a result, she could not and would not marry him and become the "queen of his home." Ruskin concluded that theology, above all else, will corrupt women away from their true calling.

In reality, what Ruskin could not accept was the fact that Rose was thinking for herself, rather than allowing him to think for her. He blamed it, instead, on the fact that she was engaged in study that was unsuited for her—theology. Ruskin was correct, however, about one thing, although he never expressed it. If women were allowed to participate in disciplines thought to be exclusively masculine, it was very likely that they would soon come to respect their own opinions as much (if not more) than men's. And this would never do.

> No feathered idol of Polynesia was ever a sign of more shameful idolatry than the modern notion . . . that the Word of God . . . may be carried about in a young lady's pocket, with tasselled ribands to mark the passages she most approves of.[72]

Apart from Ruskin's outright injunction against women studying theology, the arguments against this practice are more subtle. Religion was always an accepted outlet for women as long as it was controlled by men. However, the changing status of theology in the universities in the nineteenth century caused men to dig their heels in even deeper on this issue. First of all, theology was losing its place of prestige in the university curriculum. Near the end of the century science was making claims to being the truly masculine discipline, and an attack was waged against those who wanted to retain the dominance of the classical studies (of which theology was a part). In 1903, one professor of Engineering attacked those who wanted to maintain the study of classical literature as suffering from a lack of manliness. " 'Are you for ever to hang to the apron-strings of the ancients? Is your manhood worth so little that you cannot exist without worshipping men who were creatures like yourself?' "[73]

Intellectuals, in general, suffered attacks on their manhood. "How could the quiet man of learning be reconciled with the latter-day jungle fighter?"[74] It should not surprise us, therefore, that within the academic community itself men battled over which disciplines were "manly" and which were not. The more a discipline appeared to be a matter of purely intellectual scholarship, the more emasculated it would become. Grounded as it was in the classical tradition, theology would appear especially susceptible to such attacks.

The universities were undergoing a process of professionalization, and theology was caught up in this movement. Theology was becoming more a science and less a vocation in the university setting. Since women's affinity for religion had always been understood to be on an affective, not an intellectual level, it is quite likely that the resistance to women was, in part, due to a fear that they would emasculate the tradition. One author has noted that the battle over the female deacon-ate in the Anglican church during this period was tied to this trend toward professionalism. Prestige in the professional world is tied to theory and abstraction; to its removal from the practical world. The Church of England continued to recruit clergy from the gentleman class, and social position remained important. In order to maintain the privileged position it was necessary to conform to the dictates of the new professional ideal. "High Churchmen accepted, even courted, professionalisation. . . . Pastoral work was less important or at least less prestigious to High Churchmen; it was ideal women's work."[75]

It would seem, then, that the movement away from a pastoral orientation was occasioned by the desire to be considered a profes-sional, and because it was viewed as unmanly. Therefore, if women were to be admitted into the new profession of scientific theology, they might also contaminate this with femininity. Male theologians who already felt that their manhood was under attack strenuously sought to avoid any further suggestion that their discipline was less virile than the newer fields of science.

This fear of the feminization of religion was also apparent in other Church struggles. For example, in the early part of the twentieth century women were fighting for a larger voice in issues of Church governance. They were opposed by those who feared that if women were allowed to serve in the Representative Assembly of the Church, they would overwhelm the voice of men. After all, women constituted the largest proportion of church membership; if they were allowed authority equal with men, they might impose their own ideas. It was believed that this would detract from the power and authority of the Church.[76] In addition, men were afraid that if women were given this extra degree of authority, they would seek ordination: This fear was well-founded.[77]

The issue of ordination had a lot to do with the resistance to women in schools of theology. Up until the twentieth century degrees in theology were only awarded to those who were entering holy orders. Since women could not be ordained, there was no reason for them to study theology. One could argue that they were not discriminated against as women, but as non-ordinands, on an equal par with men. However, since there was no possibility of women becoming ordinands, this is rather circuitous.

Oxford opened its degrees to women in 1920, except for its degrees in divinity. The reason for this was the one just discussed: Women were not admitted to holy orders. However, women were not admitted to the B.D. and the D.D. until 1935,[78] and Owen Chadwick notes that these degrees were opened to any candidate (ordinands and non-ordinands alike) in 1920.[79] Since women were admitted to the university in 1920, one has to wonder why women had to wait an additional fifteen years to be granted these degrees. Cambridge opened these degrees to all candidates in 1915, but since they did not grant degrees to women until 1948, a special case cannot be made in this instance.

The movement toward professionalism in the universities in general, and theology in particular, was only a continuation of the concept of separate spheres. Professions became defined as part of the public realm (the world of men), and as a profession, theology also belonged to this sphere. The fear, in both cases, that admitting women to the male arena would emasculate it continued to provide resistance to women from both camps. Men perceived correctly that the admittance of women would change, in a fundamental way, the manner in which masculinity was defined. Their circumscribed world of power was threatened and they fought long and hard to preserve it.

[L]eading anti-feminists lived in . . . the privileged enclaves of men's colleges, men's holidays, men's professional brotherhoods, all symbolized and perpetuated in men's clubs, and they found it painful to contemplate their boyish world being invaded by the females whom their favorite institutions had deliberately, and so far successfully, excluded. . . . The all-male preserves like the universities and the professions, only perpetuated this boyish segregation.[80]

However, Gay points out that these fears were less a fear of castration than they were the fear of "being compelled to grow up,"[81] concluding, finally, that "Anti-feminism . . . was not solely a symptom of castration fears. It was a display of ignorance, of misplaced chivalry, or of a timid clinging to tradition—other kinds of fear."[82]

WOMEN AND THE NOVEL

I began this chapter by suggesting that the influence of cultural attitudes on the development of university education for women had a direct effect on the tendency of women to choose narrative as a means for expressing moral argument, and in particular as theological expression. I would now like to return to this thesis.

First of all, the developing interest in new subjects worked to move women in the direction they would take. One of the new schools to come to prominence was that of English Language and Literature. This subject had a particular appeal for women. It was not necessary to have a background in the classical languages (Latin and Greek) to excel in these subjects. Since these languages had, for the most part, been excluded from girls' education, they tended to gravitate toward subjects where this would not prove a handicap.

Also, as we have seen, English was seen as a feminine discipline. Therefore, we can expect that women were encouraged by advisors to pursue studies in this field, while being discouraged from undertaking the more masculine disciplines such as science, mathematics, and classical studies. Stearns notes that this was, in fact, the case.[83] The tendency to channel women into areas of study deemed feminine has, as we know, continued to the present day.

Nancy Armstrong has argued that the development of an educational curriculum for women was designed, originally, not to restrict women intellectually but to define specific areas of information as female. There was fear that as women began to be educated they would take in knowledge that was inappropriate for a genteel lady. Therefore, there was need for a curriculum designed especially for women. Conduct books of the late eighteenth and early nineteenth centuries, written specifically for women, delineated what were proper studies. ". . . [T]hese books distinguished a female education both from that of the male and more importantly from the classical education associated with an aristocratic tradition."[84]

However, the educated woman must be literate. Although in the early eighteenth century novels were forbidden for women because they led to romantic fantasy, by the end of the century this had changed. Certain kinds of novels were appropriate because of their capacity to both "delight and instruct." "The establishment of a female standard of taste offered a positive alternative to the male standard, which was based on the classical tradition."[85] As women began to enter the universities, then, there was already a tradition established in which literature was thought to be both appropriate and appealing to women.

Coupled with this was a long-standing tradition of women as novelists. It is a well-documented fact that writing was one area in which women could earn a living without fear of social ostracism, and that women who needed to earn an income took advantage of this. Because novels could be written within the home, and because they dealt with subjects deemed appropriate to women, "professional writing was one of the few occupations a middle class woman could pursue, in the early and mid-Victorian period, without violating the norms of appropriate feminine behavior."[86]

The notion that novel-writing was particularly fitting to women was revealed by Anthony Trollope, son of Francis Trollope. "I do not think that the writing of a novel is the most difficult task which a man may be called upon to do; but it is a task that may be supposed to demand a spirit fairly at ease."[87] Since women were supposed to be possessed of "placid and cheerful" natures, to be untroubled by, and innocent of, the concerns of the larger world, we can assume that most men believed women enjoyed a spirit "fairly at ease." Therefore, writing novels would be more natural for a woman. In addition, reading novels came to be seen as increasingly appropriate for women. As a result, the major consumers of novels were women, and it was thought fitting that women should write for other women.

However much men may have dismissed the capabilities involved in writing the novel, women took their task very seriously. It was not enough to simply tell a story in order to entertain. Women's novels tended to have a deliberate moralizing tone, and were apparently widely popular because they sold in great numbers.[88] Even romance novels, which were also extremely popular among women, had a strong moral quality. "Purity and innocence always triumphed over the powers of evil, and the story ended with a betrothal, or quite as often, with the sinner repentant on his death-bed."[89]

This idea that literature should convey a moral message was characteristic of Victorian sensibilities in general.

> The Victorian public never accepted the doctrine of art for art's sake. To the end of the century most of them retained the doctrine . . . that all art is praise. . . . Many of these writers could only justify to themselves the time spent in writing such books if the books were intended in some way to do good.[90]

Although I will discuss the novel as a vehicle for women's moral voice in more depth in the following chapter, I want to briefly consider this. As we have seen, women's seclusion in the private world was believed to protect her moral purity. Because she was not subject to the corrupting influences of the public realm, she was able to act as a mediating influence for her husband and sons. As Armstrong has argued, although the separation of spheres restricted women's social and political activity, it elevated her moral authority. Therefore, the use of the novel as a vehicle for moral argument by women would not only be in keeping with the general sensibilities of the Victorian age, but also with the ideal of true womanhood.

In a society in which women's actions were restricted and her public voice was practically nil, writing provided a way to express her opinions, her frustrations, and her fears and hopes.

> It might appear to later eyes that the early Victorian woman herself often received aliment and impulse from the very circumstances which seemed the most calculated to narrow and bend her; and the woman writers of the day added to her growing sense of strength and independence.[91]

One other point that Nancy Armstrong makes is germane to this discussion. The language that had characterized the classical tradition was one reflecting the aristocratic ideals of that tradition; it was a lofty and highly intellectual form of expression. However, this was not a style that was likely to be appealing to a general reading public not educated in a similar manner, particularly in the case of women who were excluded from the classics. The novel was much more dependent on the everyday language of the middle class, who were its primary consumers. Although this style of writing might be denigrated in an academic environment, in the world of the novel-reading public it was the form most likely to lead to commercial success. "The writing that is closest to speech places an author low in a hierarchy of writing, but is precisely the kind of English modeled on speech that identifies the well-educated woman."[92]

Much of what was written by women during this period was mediocre at best (as is much of what is written by man or woman in any age). But some of it was also very fine. The works of the Brontë sisters, George Eliot, Charlotte Yonge, and others gathered praise, however begrudgingly, from men.

> It is a melancholy fact . . . that the group of female authors is becoming every year more multitudinous and more successful. . . . Wherever we carry our successful pens we find the place preoccupied by a woman. . . .

Women have made an invasion of our legitimate domain. . . . *My* idea of
a perfect woman is one who can write, but won't.[93]

This interest in, and familiarity with, literature that women brought
with them to the universities caused them, from the very beginning, to
make up a large part of the schools in English Language and Literature. In fact, Vera Brittain notes that even after the Final Honors
School of English Language and Literature was approved in 1893,
English was for a long time considered a "woman's subject" and
looked on with disdain by men.

Narrative as a medium, then, was an interest women brought to the
universities, and was one the institutions continued to foster through
their rejection of anything perceived as feminine. At the end of *The
Women At Oxford,* Brittain includes a list of some of the more out-
standing Oxford women in nonacademic public life. It is interesting to
note that of the forty-six listed, almost two-thirds (28) became either
writers or journalists, and of these, ten were novelists.

Women also were encouraged toward the use of narrative as moral
argument by their intentional exclusion from the discipline of theology.
There is no way of knowing how many of these women might have
wanted to study theology had it been available to them. However,
many of these students were the daughters or sisters of clergymen
(perhaps due to the long-standing affiliation of the Church with these
institutions) and so it is safe to assume that many would at least have
been interested. Also, given women's training toward piety and religion, this would appear to have been a fairly natural inclination.
However, since men felt compelled to guard their territory so closely,
women were forced to find other avenues of expression.

There is at least one well-known woman who fits the picture I have
painted here: Dorothy Sayers. Sayers went to Oxford in 1912, before
the granting of degrees to women. She came from an ecclesiastical
background (her father was the headmaster of the Cathedral Choir
School at Oxford). She made her mark as a novelist of detective
fiction, and her work is generally considered some of the best, both
because of her talent as a storyteller and her keen insights into human
nature. However, in 1937 she gave up detective stories and "returned
. . . to her real love—the study of theology. . . ."[94]

Having accounted for the historical and cultural explanations that
women were more likely to write novels than other forms of literature,
I want to go on, in the next chapter, to suggest some reasons why I
think there is something inherent in narrative itself that made (and

continues to make) it a more effective vehicle of moral communication for women. I will then go on to examine the way in which Dorothy Sayers employed narrative as a forum for moral argument, and finally to consider this method, from a feminist perspective, in light of current discussions regarding narrative theology.

NOTES

1. For a detailed account of the struggle for degrees at Cambridge see Rita McWilliams-Tullberg, *Women at Cambridge* (London: Victor Gollancz Ltd., 1975). For an account of the experiences of women at Oxford see Vera Brittain, *The Women at Oxford: A Fragment of History* (London: George G. Harrap & Co., Ltd., 1960); also Annie M. A. H. Rogers, *Degrees by Degrees* (Great Britain: Oxford University Press, 1938).

2. McWilliams-Tullberg, *Women at Cambridge;* 40.

3. V. H. H. Green, *Religion at Oxford and Cambridge* (London: SCM Press, Ltd., 1964), 11.

4. McWilliams-Tullberg, *Women at Cambridge,* 14.

5. Brittain, *Women at Oxford,* 41; McWilliams-Tullberg, *Women at Cambridge,* 43. For a thorough discussion of the issue of celibacy at Oxford see A. J. Engel, *From Clergyman to Don* (Oxford: Clarendon Press, 1983), especially 106–14. Although C. P. Snow's *The Masters* (New York: Charles Scribner's Sons, 1951), is a novel, and therefore a "fictional" portrayal of academic life in 1937, it nevertheless demonstrates that masculine influence still dominated the university at this time.

6. Brittain, *Women at Oxford,* 107.

7. Brittain, *Women at Oxford,* 109.

8. Brittain, *Women at Oxford,* 21.

9. Green, *Religion at Oxford,* 13.

10. Ibid., 12.

11. Ibid., 13.

12. Rogers, *Degrees by Degrees,* 11.

13. Peter Gay, *The Bourgeois Experience: Victoria to Freud,* vol. 1, *Education of the Senses* (New York and Oxford: Oxford University Press, 1984), 170.

14. Brittain, *Women at Oxford,* 30.

15. McWilliams-Tullberg, *Women at Cambridge,* 48.

16. McWilliams-Tullberg, *Women at Cambridge,* 42–43.

17. Brittain, *Women at Oxford,* 154–5. Cambridge also required chaperons for its female students; McWilliams-Tullberg, *Women at Cambridge,* 71.

18. John Ruskin, "Of Queen's Gardens," in *Essays and Letters Selected from the Writings of John Ruskin,* ed. Mrs. Louis G. Hufford (Boston: Ginn & Company, 1894), 90.

19. Deborah Gorham, *The Victorian Girl and the Feminine Ideal* (Bloomington: Indiana University Press, 1982), 90.

20. The article that Dr. Anderson was responding to can be found, in part, in chapter one.

21. Elizabeth Garrett Anderson, "Sex and Mind in Education: A Reply," *Fortnightly Review* (May 1874), cited in Susan Groag Bell and Karen M. Offen, eds., *Women, the Family, and Freedom: The Debate in Documents*, vol. 1, 1750–1880 (Stanford, Calif.: Stanford University Press, 1983), 434.

22. Gorham, *Victorian Girl*, 91.

23. Brittain, *Women at Oxford*, 35.

24. Brittain, *Women at Oxford*, 35–6; McWilliams-Tullberg, *Women at Cambridge*, 24–31.

25. McWilliams-Tullberg, *Women at Cambridge*, 39.

26. M. Burrows, "Female Education," *Quarterly Review* 126 (1869), cited in Patricia Hollis, *Women in Public 1850–1900: Documents of the Victorian Women's Movement* (London: George Allen & Unwin, 1979), 144–45.

27. Gay, *Bourgeois Experience*, 194.

28. Gorham, *Victorian Girl*, 109.

29. Rogers, *Degrees by Degrees*, 18–19. The speaker was Dean John Burgeon, and Rogers reports "the congregation laughed aloud" at the end of his sermon. Nevertheless, the sermon was published and no doubt reflected the views of many men and women of this time.

30. Rogers, *Degrees by Degrees*, 20.

31. Rogers, *Degrees by Degrees*, 52.

32. Herbert Spencer, *The Principles of Sociology* (1893), cited in Bell and Offen, eds., *Women, the Family*, 414.

33. For a thorough accounting of the changes that Oxford underwent see A. J. Engel. For a discussion that includes Cambridge see V. H. H. Green, and also Owen Chadwick, "The Universities," in Owen Chadwick, *The Victorian Church*, part 2 (London: Adam & Charles Black, Ltd., 1970), 439–61.

34. Engel, *From Clergyman to Don*, 4.

35. Chadwick, *Victorian Church*, 439.

36. Chadwick, *Victorian Church*, 441.

37. Chadwick, *Victorian Church*, 439; Engel, *From Clergyman to Don*, 56; Green, *Religion at Oxford*, 297.

38. Green, *Religion at Oxford*, 297.

39. Green, *Religion at Oxford*, 18.

40. Engel's book is a study of this move to professionalization at Oxford, and Chadwick, in *Victorian Church* notes this as a phenomenon at both universities, 439–61.

41. Engel, *From Clergyman to Don*, 12.

42. Chadwick, *Victorian Church*, 450.

43. Peter N. Stearns, *Be A Man!* (New York: Holmes & Meier Publishers, Inc., 1979), 97–98.

44. Engel, *From Clergyman to Don,* 14–54.

45. Brittain, *Women at Oxford,* 40.

46. Green, *Religion at Oxford,* 297–307.

47. Engel, *From Clergyman to Don,* 273–74; Green, *Religion at Oxford,* 305.

48. Chadwick, *Victorian Church,* 450.

49. Chadwick notes this occurred at Cambridge in 1915 and at Oxford in 1920; see also Green, *Religion at Oxford,* 340–45.

50. McWilliams-Tullberg, *Women at Cambridge,* 199–200.

51. Green, *Religion at Oxford,* 346.

52. Gay, *Bourgeois Experience,* 194.

53. Stearns, *Be A Man!,* 112.

54. Gay, *Bourgeois Experience,* 197. Gay's work has been criticized for its "porous Freudianism" by Erica Harth in her review of *The Bourgeois Experience,* by Peter Gay, in *Science and Society* 48 (Fall 1984): 376–79. Harth goes on to say that "Freudian discourse has not acknowledged its own class-bound character, and Gay's use of it remains blandly uncritical." Jeffrey Weeks has made a similar critique, noting that "Gay's rigid Freudian orthodoxy" does not allow him to deal dispassionately with his subject; Jeffrey Weeks, "An Anxious Sensibility," review of *The Bourgeois Experience* by Peter Gay, in *History Today* 34 (August 1984): 54. Elaine Showalter has noted that Gay's Freudian approach "often neglects realities and circumstances that suggest a more limited thesis than his"; Elaine Showalter "Marriage Victorian-Style," review of *The Bourgeois Experience* by Peter Gay, in *The Nation* 238 (24 March 1984): 356–59. However, while acknowledging the problems inherent in Gay's approach, the argument that he makes regarding the perception of women as a threat, and the suggestion that the construct of woman as destroyer is a reaction to the idea of woman as angel is one that is articulated by others who are not dependent on Freud, and one that I think is borne up by literature of the period.

55. Gay, *Bourgeois Experience,* 200–01.

56. Gay, *Bourgeois Experience,* 201.

57. Nina Auerbach, *Woman and the Demon: The Life of a Victorian Myth* (Cambridge, Mass.: Harvard University Press, 1982), 108.

58. Gay, *Bourgeois Experience,* 207.

59. Auerbach, *Women and the Demon,* 186.

60. Brittain, *Women at Oxford,* 107.

61. McWilliams-Tullberg, *Women at Cambridge,* 108.

62. McWilliams-Tullberg, *Women at Cambridge,* 119.

63. McWilliams-Tullberg, *Women at Cambridge,* 193.

64. McWilliams-Tullberg, *Women at Cambridge,* 90.

65. Margaret Maison, " 'Thine, Only Thine!' Women Hymn Writers in Britain, 1760–1835," in *Religion in the Lives of English Women,* ed. Gail Malmgreen (Bloomington: Indiana University Press, 1986), 11–40.

66. Gail Malmgreen, ed., *Religion in the Lives of English Women* (Bloomington: Indiana University Press, 1986), 5.

67. Brian Heeney, "The Beginnings of Church Feminism: Women and the Councils of the Church of England, 1879–1919," in *Religion in the Lives of English Women,* ed. Gail Malmgreen (Bloomington: Indiana University Press, 1986), 260.

68. Ruskin, "Of Queen's Gardens," 87.

69. J. A. Hobson, *John Ruskin: Social Reformer* (Boston: Dana Estes & Company, 1898), 291–92.

70. R. H. Wilenski, *John Ruskin: An Introduction to Further Study of His Life and Work* (New York: Russell & Russell, 1933), 349.

71. Ibid., 82–85.

72. John Ruskin, *Aratra Pentelici, II* (1870), cited in Wilenski, *John Ruskin,* 350.

73. Engel, *From Clergyman to Don,* 226.

74. Stearns, *Be A Man!,* 101.

75. Catherine M. Prelinger, "The Female Deaconate in the Anglican Church: What Kind of Ministry for Women," in *Religion in the Lives of English Women,* ed. Gail Malmgreen (Bloomington: Indiana University Press, 1986), 185.

76. Heeney, "Church Feminism," 278.

77. Heeney, "Church Feminism," 280.

78. Brittain, *Women at Oxford,* 151.

79. Chadwick, *Victorian Church,* 453.

80. Gay, *Bourgeois Experience,* 208.

81. Gay, *Bourgeois Experience,* 208.

82. Gay, *Bourgeois Experience,* 212.

83. Stearns, *Be A Man!,* 100.

84. Nancy Armstrong, *Desire and Domestic Fiction: A Political History of the Novel* (New York: Oxford University Press, 1987), 102–03.

85. Armstrong, *Desire and Domestic Fiction,* 103.

86. Gorham, *Victorian Girl,* 135.

87. Janet Dunbar, *The Early Victorian Woman: Some Aspects of Her Life (1837–57)* (London: George C. Harrap & Co., Ltd., 1953), 124.

88. Dunbar, *Early Victorian,* 120–21.

89. Dunbar, *Early Victorian,* 122.

90. Chadwick, *Victorian Church,* 462–63.

91. Dunbar, *Early Victorian,* 131.

92. Armstrong, *Desire and Domestic Fiction,* 149.

93. Dunbar, *Early Victorian,* 131–32.

94. Brittain, *Women at Oxford,* 124.

3

The Structure of the Novel and Women's Narrative Voice

In previous chapters I identified certain cultural and social assumptions regarding women that were conducive to the emergence of women as novelists in the nineteenth century. Essentially I have argued that the reigning paradigm of separate spheres, while restricting women's social participation, did grant women an authoritative voice in the articulation of private moral values. I then considered the ways in which, as women began to enter the universities, this concept of "woman's nature," coupled with structural and curricular changes, made degrees in modern languages and literature more accessible to women while degrees in theology were closed to them. As a result, women's theological voice tended to find expression in a narrative construct.

I now want to address one further issue before I go on to examine the narrative and theological work of Dorothy Sayers, and the implication of this for a feminist methodology of narrative theology. The question I want to consider concerns the development of the genre itself. Are there intrinsic characteristics of the novel that make it particularly effective as a tool for women's moral argument? To answer this question it is necessary to look not only at the categories of the genre but also at the historical context in which it evolved. I obviously cannot do full justice to this discussion, but I want to look at certain aspects of its development that I think are particularly significant for an understanding of women's narrative voice.

The assumption I begin with is that literature does not develop devoid of a context, and that the development of literary forms implies certain ways of viewing the world and the self in relation to the world. As one critic has noted, "Most theories of the nature of literature are more or less concealed theories of the nature of man [sic] and of the good society. In this sense, literary thinking is inseparable from moral and social thinking."[1] What I want to ascertain in discussing the historical development of the novel is what kinds of questions it might be best suited to address, and the significance of this for women.

Ian Watt's *The Rise of the Novel* has stood for over thirty years as the classic study of the novel. Watt focused his study on the writings of three novelists of the eighteenth century—Defoe, Richardson, and Fielding—whom he regarded as the first three novelists proper in English literature.[2] He believed that the fact that all three appeared within a single generation was more than a mere coincidence; according to Watt the conditions of the times were favorable to their genius.[3] In delineating what the conditions of the times were, he focused in particular on two aspects: "formal realism" and "the rise of the middle class."

Watt maintained that the eighteenth century evoked a new concept of human nature and that this was reflected in new literary styles. Change in literature is related to change in "the way men [sic] think and react to life, both as groups and as individuals."[4] The key, then, to understanding the development of new literary forms is not to be found in the literature itself, but in the world that gives it birth. According to Watt, the eighteenth century was marked by a new focus on the individual, and this led to the development of a narrative form that demanded realistic representation.

To clarify what he meant, Watt drew a parallel between the development of the novel and contemporary movements in philosophical thought. Watt argued that the rise of the novel corresponded with the rejection of classical philosophical ideals of universals. Modern philosophical realism maintained that truth could be discovered by an individual through the senses. Citing Descartes, Watt pointed to the shift in understanding truth as a wholly individual matter and thought that the novel was the literary form that best reflected this changing paradigm. "Previous literary forms had reflected the general tendency of their cultures to make conformity to traditional practice the major test of truth."[5] In the novel the main criterion for truth was not conformity to universal ideals of truth, but rather individual experience.

The changes in both philosophy and literature were indicative, according to Watt, of a larger change in Western civilization that replaced a vision of the world as a unified whole with a vision of the world as "a developing but unplanned aggregate of particular individuals having particular experiences at particular times and at particular places."[6] He used the term "formal realism" to describe the basic character of the novel, and claimed it was a premise that was implicit in the novel itself.

> . . . [T]he novel is a full and authentic report of human experience, and is therefore under an obligation to satisfy its reader with such details of the story . . . presented through a more largely referential use of language than is common in other literary forms.[7]

According to Watt, the formal realism of the novel made it particularly well suited to address the interests of the individual who was the new focus of social concern.

Watt also assumed the existence of a middle class, who understood themselves as such, to whom the novel was addressed and for whom it became the vehicle of expression. According to his hypothesis, with the growth of a new middle class in eighteenth-century England there was an increasingly literate population who became the new consumers of literature. Corresponding to the growth of literacy was the expanding number of those who were able to afford the cost of books. As a result of these influences, Watt noted that more people were reading exclusively for pleasure than ever before and this weakened the importance of classical and modern letters.[8] As the middle class became increasingly the main audience for this new literature, their tastes came to have a determining influence on what was written and published. Indeed, Watt contended that the burgeoning middle class "may have altered the centre of gravity of the reading public sufficiently to place the middle class as a whole in a dominating position for the first time."[9]

While not wishing to discredit the contributions Ian Watt made to a modern understanding of the development of the novel, more recent analyses of this subject have suggested that the causal relationship that Watt articulates suffers from oversimplification, and that a more nuanced approach might provide a better understanding of the complexities surrounding the emergence of novelistic narrative. In terms of Watt's identification of formal realism as the determining characteristic of the novel, critics have noted that the early novelists (Defoe, Richardson, and Fielding, in particular) continued to draw on "stock situations and conventions" of the Romance, which Watt thought they had replaced. There also continued to be, according to Michael Mc-

Keon, an outpouring of literature that continued the "anti-individualist and idealizing tradition of romance."[10] So, although Watt claims that realism is the distinguishing characteristic of the novel, the early novels did not fully satisfy this criterion.

Additionally, Watt presupposes an existent middle class that called the novel into being. Critics, however, point out that in the early eighteenth century there is no clearly identifiable middle class; it exists at best in a nascent form.[11] If the novel was a response to the middle-class ideology, and yet there was no well-defined ideology, how can we account for its development? Indeed, Nancy Armstrong argues that the novel did not arise in response to middle-class demands, but rather that it was the forum through which the middle class conceptualized itself.[12]

There is one additional issue that Watt failed to address that is critical to my study, and this is the dominance of the novel by women. Armstrong points out that an explanation of this phenomenon is lacking in any history of the English novel. Watt fell back on the oversimplification of "female sensibility" as being better suited to concerns of the novel. His explanation of the novel failed, in this respect, "because—to a man—history is represented as the history of male institutions . . . [and] leaves all the truly interesting questions unasked. . . ."[13] Watt, and others, presupposed a world divided by gender, and therefore did not ask how this world might have come to be and how the novel might have contributed to its formation.[14] I will address Armstrong's analysis in more depth at a later point, but now want to return to McKeon.

A DIALECTICAL THEORY OF GENRE FORMATION

If Watt's account of the emergence of the novel suffers from over-generalization, how can we achieve a better understanding? McKeon suggests that a dialectical theory of genre formation might be appropriate. Extrapolating from Marx, McKeon claims that fundamental to historical life is "the inseparability of diverse social formations within the dialectical continuum of history. . . ."[15] The English novel did not suddenly appear as a new form in history; rather its origins occur at the end of a long history of "novelistic useage."[16] In fact, the ability to identify the novel as a specific form is possible only in retrospect, once certain narrative conventions are well enough established to identify it as a particular genre.

By the middle of the eighteenth century, the stabilizing of terminology—
the increasing acceptance of "the novel" as a canonic term, so that
contemporaries can "speak of it as *such*"—signals the stability of the
conceptual category and of the class of literary products that it encloses.[17]

To understand the novel, then, we cannot simply look at its location
in history when it is clearly identifiable and assume that there was
something unique about that moment that enabled its emergence. The
development of the genre must be understood in terms of the processes
that formed it. Both McKeon and Armstrong see its development as a
literary correlate to social changes that were occurring in England in
the seventeenth and eighteenth centuries. These changes were due to
the movement away from the ideological predominance of an aristocratic nobility and its gradual replacement by a gentry or middle class
based not on lineage and landed interests but on individual qualities of
the mind and monied interests. The emergence of the novel should not
be placed at the end of this transformation, but should be understood
as part of the process and as a mediating form that enabled such
changes to proceed without social collapse or chaos.

According to McKeon the novel must be understood as a " 'simple
abstraction,' a deceptively monolithic category that encloses a complex historical process."[18] The novel attained its stability and influence
when it did because of its power to conceptualize and articulate
problems that were central to early modern experience. These were
problems of categorical instability of two kinds. The first related to
generic categories, which McKeon calls "questions of truth," and that
reflected "a major cultural transition in attitudes toward how to tell the
truth in narrative."[19] These questions are the reflection of an epistemological crisis. The second group related to social categories and
reflected a "crisis in attitudes toward how the external social order is
related to the internal, moral state of its members."[20] These he refers
to as questions of virtues. Both categories of questions pose problems
of signification. What kind of authority signifies truth in narrative and
what kind of social behavior signifies an individual's virtue?

The novel is able to confront both the epistemological and social
crises simultaneously, and is therefore able to mediate the process of
transition. Questions of truth and virtue are more manageable when
they are seen as analagous, and the novel serves an explanatory
function in doing this. In fact, says McKeon, this analogy "is the
foundation of the novel."[21]

As it related to epistemological changes, the development of the novel is part of the process of secularization.[22] Prior to the seventeenth century, the claim to truth rested on received authorities and tradition. But with the advent of scientific inquiry, truth begins to rely on empirical validation. McKeon traces the epistemological crisis through "naive empiricism" as a reaction against traditionalism, and then to "extreme skepticism," which both reacted against and subverted empiricism.

He notes that questions of truth in narrative undergo similar transitions as narrative discourse moves from Romance as a received tradition, which is therefore authoritative, to the incorporation of claims to historicity as empirical validation of truth, to skepticism as to whether any fiction can claim to be true. His analysis makes clear that narrative conventions were part of a broader epistemological transition, and that it was continually subjected to and refined by, and contributed to, prevailing conceptions of understanding. "Theory develops in dialectical relation to genre as a supplementary discourse of detached commentary that is yet inseparable, in its own development, from the corollary process of genre formation."[23]

Doctrines of literary realism arose from the ruins of the claims to historicity and validated literary creations for being not history, but history-like. No longer making objective claims to empirical validation, they nevertheless claimed to be true in that they reflect human experience in an authentic way.

> . . . [I]t is only by virtue of a complete and implicit assent to the empirical notion of truth as the evidence of the senses that modern culture became sufficiently tolerant of artful fictions to pass beyond the bare recognition of their incredibility and to conceive the possibility of their validation in other terms. . . . The novel, once established, maintained its domination of the field by incorporating that solution within its own conception of truth as realism.[24]

Realism is not, as Watt seemed to indicate, an accepted and uncontested mode of knowledge, which then develops as the novel in a literary incarnation. It is, rather, the outcome of a narrative evolution that is part of an overall epistemological movement; an evolution that is as much the process of a realistic vision as it is the product.

Questions of virtue undergo a corollary transition.[25] Again beginning with the late sixteenth century, McKeon notes that the prevailing ideology was an aristocratic one in which the concept of honor was both internal and external. The social order was neither circumstantial or arbitrary, but corresponded to an internal moral order. Honor, or virtue, was an inherited characteristic. The gradual discrediting of aristocratic honor as the locus of virtue was accompanied by a breakdown of fictions that no longer satisfied the ideological ends they were designed to serve.[26]

As early as the sixteenth century there were signs that indicated a growing discord about the social hierarchy that characterized England.[27] By the end of the seventeenth century the social conflict was between landed interests and monied interests, and by the eighteenth century "middle class" values had transformed an aristocracy that still retained the shell of the status model.[28] "The social significance of the English novel at the time of its origins lies in its ability to mediate—to represent as well as contain—the revolutionary clash between status and class orientations and the attendent crisis of status inconsistency."[29]

Just as naive empiricism was a reaction against traditionalism, and extreme skepticism a subversion of empiricism in the epistemological arena, the social crisis was accompanied by similar transitions. Against the social injustice of the aristocratic ideology there developed a "progressive ideology," which maintained that virtue is not prescribed by status but is demonstrated by achievement. In reaction to the progressive ideology arose the "conservative ideology" with its critique of a new aristocracy as undeserving. For conservatives, the monied interests were inseparable from the progressive ideology, and they saw this as a quantification of virtue; money and power without merit.

> . . . [I]t is the curse of modernity to have divided personality from prescribed status. . . . The rule of the absolute prince was gradually being usurped by the rule of the private individual and his absolute right to choose his leaders and dispose of his property according to the dictates of his natural appetites.[30]

Narrative was particularly well suited for representing these opposing ideologies, claims McKeon, due to the fact that questions of virtue "have an inherently narrative focus because they are concerned with . . . how human capacity is manifested in and through time."[31] As a genre, the Romance served the aristocratic ideology because at its heart this ideology affirmed the idea that a stable social order was indicative of a greater moral order, and that social order was dependent on genealogy. The Romance, which depended on received authority and tradition for its validation of truth, celebrated this conviction.

However, as this ideology disintegrated, a new narrative model developed; one that had the capacity not only to address itself to the changing ideologies but to mediate the change. This new model reflected a sociohistorical understanding of competing social claims, shifting the locus of truth from tradition to experience.

Narrative forms changed as epistemological convictions and social reality changed. But they did not represent a radical disjuncture from preceding conditions and convictions. Rather, they served to mediate between conflicting conceptions and to enable transition. The formation of the novelistic narrative was dependent on historical experience itself, but literary models both structured the way history was experienced and at the same time were formed by that experience.

The development of the novel, then, was not a response to a changed social world in eighteenth-century England, but was in fact one of the forces that brought about the changes that eventually gave rise to the middle class. It did not simply mirror the values of a new class, but also helped create and establish those values as they gained authority. It would be fair to say that the novel was the vehicle through which the middle class created itself, and as such it was a political force.

The novel mediated the gradual shift from the authority of received tradition to the authority of individual experience. The model of the autonomous individual that eventually triumphed in the nineteenth century, and the realism that came to mark modern literature, developed in corollary fashion. Society was slowly separated from self, and the eventual view of society as impinging on the individual signified the autonomy of the individual.

> The autonomy of the self consists in its capacity to enter into largely negative relation with the society it vainly conceives itself to have created, to resist its encroachments and to be constructed by them. The work of the novel after 1820 is increasingly to record this struggle.[32]

THE GENDERING OF VIRTUE

It is in relationship to this creation of the modern concept of the individual that Nancy Armstrong addresses her examination of the domestic novel. Like McKeon, she also sees the novel as part of the process of social change and understands it not as a response to a middle-class ideology, but as the central factor in the creation of that ideology. For her, this process cannot be separated from the social construction of the domestic woman. She argues that the category of domesticity is antecedent to the novel, and that the modern novel exists because of this change. The rise of the middle class, therefore, did not call the novel into being; the novel established the middle-class consciousness.

In her treatment of the novel she argues three basic points. First, that sexuality is a cultural construct and therefore has a history. Second, that written representations of the self allowed the modern individual to become an economic and psychological reality. Finally, that the modern individual was first and foremost a woman. "I will insist that one cannot distinguish the production of the new female ideal either from the rise of the novel or from the rise of the new middle classes in England."[33] The formation of the modern State in England was the result of cultural hegemony, and the strategies of representation expressed by the novel revised the common understanding of individual identity.

Drawing on the work of Michael Foucault in *The History of Sexuality*, she argues that it is "possible to consider sexual relations as the site for changing power relations between classes and cultures as well as between genders and generations."[34] This is possible if sexuality is understood as a purely semiotic process, which includes the gendering of our world according to masculine and feminine attributes. Gender, therefore, has a history. Her work seeks to demonstrate that gender differences "came to dominate the functions of generation and genealogy, which organized an earlier culture."[35]

Armstrong's study begins at about the point where McKeon leaves off—the end of the eighteenth century, when the concept of the individual begins to become the increasing focus of narrative fiction. As does McKeon, she understands the role of the novel as providing a mediation of the transition from a landed aristocracy to a monied middle class as the social paradigm.

With the aristocratic ideology questions of virtue were tied to status, which was dependent on genealogy. The value of the person depended on one's place in the social order and was inherently a political category. How, then, was the shift to merit based on individual qualities of the mind, ostensibly devoid of political implications, accomplished? Armstrong argues this occurred through the displacement of the model of the social contract espoused by modern liberalism by a sexual contract model as the narrative paradigm. The novel represented social conflict as personal history and thereby appeared to remove it from the political arena. "By virtue of their apparent

disregard for matters that were supposed to concern men, plots turning
on the sexual contract offered the means of passing off ideology as the
product of purely human concern.''[36] Although McKeon does not deal
extensively with the issue of sexuality in the formation of the novel,
he does acknowledge the way in which virtue came to be associated
with concepts of gender.[37]

According to Armstrong, the domestic novel removed the struggle
of competing class values from the political realm and translated them
to the private world, as a struggle between the sexes. The shift in the
delineation of moral categories that occurred in the eighteenth century
has been noted by other analysts of the novel. ''It is . . . very evident
that the eighteenth century witnessed a tremendous narrowing of the
ethical scale, a redefinition of virtue in primarily sexual terms.''[38]
Virtue became individualized, losing its political character. This can
be clearly seen, says Armstrong, in Richardson's novel *Pamela,* where
the refusal of a young serving girl to acquiesce to the will of her master
is translated from a clash between classes to the struggle of individual
wills.[39]

The concept of the domestic woman, which became paradigmatic
for middle-class ideology and was the focus of the domestic novel, had
its roots in the conduct books written for women in the eighteenth
century. Until the early eighteenth century, different levels of society
had different ideas about what made a woman marriageable, but by the
second half of this century the ideal of womanhood proposed by these
conduct books had passed into the ''domain of common sense'' and
provided a frame of reference for the novel.[40] This model, the domestic
angel, was discussed in my first chapter.

Within the framework of the earlier aristocratic model, a woman's
desirability in marriage was directly tied to her social status. Class
barriers were clearly defined, and marriage served a political function.
However, conduct books began to redefine the desirability of a woman
on the basis of qualities of the mind, not lineage. These conduct books
were aimed at those who defined themselves as neither aristocracy nor
working class, and as they redefined the desirability of women, they
helped to establish the identity of this class. According to Armstrong,
conduct books helped to create an idea of the middle class before it
actually existed. ''If there is any truth in this, then it is also reasonable
to claim that the modern individual was first and foremost a female.''[41]

The creation of a concept of personal value that was removed from
political position was first articulated in relation to women. It was
situated in the realm of the private household, which became the

domain of women, and which women were supposed to define and control. The conduct books created a concept of domesticity that came to have increasing influence in society and that eventually became the paradigmatic model for the nineteenth century.

> In bringing into being a concept of the household on which socially hostile groups felt they could all agree, the domestic ideal helped create the fiction of horizontal affiliations that only a century later could be said to have materialized as an economic reality.[42]

As the ideal of the conduct books became the generally accepted model of desirability for women, their influence decreased and they were replaced by the domestic novel. Because the idea of domesticity was represented by women, these novels focused increasingly on women, and therefore gave rise to women novelists. Women's lives and women's voices developed an authority they had heretofore lacked. If virtue was dependent on individual qualities of the mind and heart, and if these qualities were developed outside the realm of public life (in the domestic household), women, who ruled this domain, become the model of the new self. In reference, again, to *Pamela,* Armstrong points out: "If a servant girl could claim possession of herself as her own first property, then virtually any individual must similarly have a self to withhold or give in a modern form of exchange within the state."[43] She goes on to say that "It is no ordinary moment in literary history when a male novelist imagines a woman . . . [who] has the power to reform the male of the dominant class."[44]

In the process of redefining women's desirability, the novel also helped to redefine the value of the individual in the modern State. As gender assumed priority over other differences, and as the struggle between classes was redefined in terms of the narrative paradigm of the struggle between the sexes, a new political world emerged, "composed not of races, classes, or even genders, but of individuals. . . ."[45] Over time the novel produced a new language that enabled the examination and understanding of individual lives as meaningful for others. But the novel was not so much a response to a new concept of the individual as it was the process by which this individual self was delineated and developed.

THE PARADOX OF WOMAN'S VOICE

Both McKeon and Armstrong have identified the novel as a mediating force in the processes of epistemological and social change that marked England in the seventeenth and eighteenth centuries. This was a movement in which an aristocratic class and the identification of truth with the authority of tradition was subverted by the emergence of a dominant middle class and the location of truth in the individual experience of the self. Nancy Armstrong has further identified this change as directly related to the gendering of virtue that occurred with the establishment of the domestic ideal.

The result was that by the nineteenth century the concept of separate spheres was firmly entrenched as a new ideological model in England. The lives of men and women were marked by a radical disjuncture in terms of their spheres of influence and authority. The moral authority of women was dependent on their absence from the public world, yet it was through this redefining of authority that a new public model of political authority was established. Additionally, although women's place was defined as antithetical to public life, as the novel increasingly became the vehicle for moral debate women's voice came to have a corresponding public influence. This is the paradoxical nature of women's narrative voice: The novel, which firmly established woman as a private entity, was the same vehicle through which she would gain a public voice.

In light of these changes, what implications might be drawn for a contemporary understanding of women's narrative voice? I want to focus on three specific aspects of the changing narrative paradigm, all of which begin with the understanding of the political function of the novel: the emergent concept of the individual and the shift in the locus of authority, the role of women as a moral authority, and finally the ability of the novel to mediate between public and private interests.

The Individual and Authority

The development of the modern novel was part of a process of epistemological change in which the authority of tradition was usurped by the authority of the individual and the corresponding social dominance of the aristocratic class was gradually replaced by the middle class. This changing paradigm was significant in the lives of women. When authority was restricted to status as a political category, women had no authority. As both McKeon and Armstrong make clear, status was defined on the basis of a patrilineal genealogy. The status of women was derivative, by attachment through marriage or birth to a male-centered social structure.

However, as status categories began to disintegrate as the locus of authority a new basis for truth, the experience of the individual, became the ground for authority. The development of the novel helped to create this new paradigm and then celebrated it. The private experiences of the individual and the moral implications that the author attached to these became an end in themselves.[46]

The novel created a world view in which the relationships between individual persons became definitive for exploring the meaning and purpose of life. The particulars of common life came to be imbued with a moral meaning and import that had not before been imaginable. In a world where real life was the life of the aristocracy, the life of the average person had little, if any, social significance, and could not be thought of as instructive for the general community. However, as the value of each individual life, divorced from status categories, gained in importance, the examination of these lives could provide the basis for moral instruction. If the individual, as individual, is the center of the universe, then individual actions take on universal significance. As a result, novelists came to have

> an intensely active conception of life as a continuous moral and social struggle; they all see every event in ordinary life as proposing an intrinsically moral issue on which reason and conscience must be exerted to the full before right action is possible.[47]

The moral meanings of one's actions are defined not in terms of one's place in society as defined by class, but in terms of individual qualities of the mind. They are defined in relationship to society, but in tension with the actions of other individuals in the community.

Since individual experience came to take on new meaning, women's lives could be examined in this new context; the particular experiences of women's lives gained new validity and meaning. If truth is revealed through the individual experience of life, then truth can be found in the life experiences of women, no matter how greatly they differed from the life experiences of men.

The focus on the individual also presented the possibility for new freedom of self-expression for women. This was the case not only for the development of women characters in novels, but also for women as novelists. In their writing these women laid claim to the right to be heard as individual women with individual voices. Inga-Stina Ewbank, in her study of the Brontë sisters, notes that the fundamental issue of nineteenth-century feminism was a struggle for autonomy. "In this sense each of the Brontës is a feminist rejecting a collective classification as a 'female novelist,' claiming an autonomous personality as a writer."[48]

The focus on the individual, then, paved the way for the development of a political persona for women. In a culture defined by status, and where women had little status independent of men, they remained essentially invisible. What it meant to be a real person was to be male. Literature within such a culture by and large reflected male reality, and women who figured in such literature were subject to male definition.

Modern theorists taking a sociology of knowledge approach have noted the implications of this perspective for women. Essentially, the theoretical basis of this approach is that our understanding of the nature of reality is conditioned (although not entirely determined) by the social and historical contexts within which we live.

> The fundamental issues of the sociology of knowledge perspective are to understand how ideas reproduce our definitions of social reality, who produces ideas, under what conditions ideas are made, and the consequences of ideas and beliefs that, in the case of sexism, systematically define women in stereotypical and distorted terms.[49]

Needless to say, as long as men controlled the definition and dissemination of knowledge within society, the concerns of women's lives, which were so far removed from the lives of men, were given little, if any, attention. This led, as modern feminists have noted, to the phenomenon of women being "written out of history."

However, the changing focus of the novel brought not only women's lives as subject but also women as authors into the public eye, and there was a tendency for literature to become "a primarily feminine pursuit."[50] According to Elaine Showalter, within a century women had gone from being newcomers on the literary scene to being one of the major forces in English literature. Indeed, she notes that many critics thought "the nineteenth century was the Age of the Female Novelist."[51]

I am not claiming that women gained, as a result of the novel, control of the public, political realm. The separation of spheres in Victorian England remained a determining factor and continued to define women in terms of domesticity. What I do think important is that the emphasis of the novel on the individual made the private lives of women (and men) part of public debate and as such gave women an identity that they had lacked before. "Because women have been written, they have become visible as such, and writing as women has made it possible for a distinctively female voice to be heard."[52]

Woman as Moral Authority

As Armstrong has made clear, the novel helped to create the concept of the private sphere. However, unlike many modern feminist analysts, she does not think that this meant women were devoid of power. In fact, she suggests that viewing the public realm as the only arena of political power is a particularly masculine perspective. She argues that the private world, which was dominated by women in the nineteenth century, was the new locus of moral authority, and that as a result, women's moral voice gained a new power.

The new role of women as a moral authority cannot be separated from the emergence of the individual as the reigning paradigm. If each person has value, then the conflicting claims of persons existing within society have moral significance, and the way these conflicts are resolved provide moral lessons. The tendency of nineteenth-century novels, in general, to be characterized by a heavy-handed moralizing was discussed in chapter two. Samuel Pickering notes that "the great tradition of the early nineteenth-century English novel is the moral tradition. . . . Evangelical standards became the primary critical yardstick by which English Christian readers measured literature."[53] Ewbank cautions her readers that "We need . . . constantly to remind ourselves of the preference of the age for practical—moral rather than aesthetic—merits in fiction. . . ."[54]

Virtue was privatized, and since the private world of family, home, and relationships was, by and large, the boundary of women's existence, questions within this sphere were especially important for women, and women were thought to have particular authority in relationship to them. "Morality dwells above all in kindness and consideration within family relationships; the identity of women lies in her moral function as daughter, sister, wife and mother."[55] Although women's lives were restricted by the boundaries of the domestic household, within these limits moral questions could be addressed.

Patricia Meyer Spacks observed that when men act and women submit, "the question is what—or who—she submits to, why and how she suffers and loves."[56] In most women's novels the plot revolved not so much around a woman's attempt to break free of her traditional role as it did around her efforts to cope within it. Or, according to Spacks, it was not so much a question of what she was capable of doing with her life as it was an examination of what she was capable of being. If society dictated that a women must live in a role submissive to a man, then what were the moral implications in the way she played that role? "Where today we think of personal decisions concerning family education, work and sexuality primarily in psychological terms, in Victorian England the same conflicts were understood primarily as moral problems."[57]

If a woman had no option but to choose a husband in order to have some life of her own, then the man she chose and the reasons behind her choice became a moral choice. If the only area where she could exercise her creative abilities was in the bearing and rearing of children, then how she raised those children became a moral responsibility. It was in the way in which she did what she had no choice but to do that the characters of these novels worked out their own selfhood.

The rise of the novel reflects the increasing emphasis on personal morality, and this is articulated in sexual relationships for both men and women, especially in the middle class. What is significant for women in this shift is that with the elevation of the private to a new level of ethical consideration women became moral agents within the limits of their cultural restrictions. When the formation of virtue had been joined to the public arena, and women were banned from participation in this, they were necessarily excluded from moral development as it was understood. However with the privatization of morality for both men and women, woman's moral voice gained new authority. In fact, as the central figure of the private sphere, women could claim to have special insight into this arena, and, as Armstrong argues, gained moral authority as a result.

Women novelists understood, and took seriously, their role as "educators of the heart," according to Showalter. In their work they sought to introduce feminine values (the private sphere) into the masculine world, or the public realm, and suggested in doing so that there were contributions they could make to men's moral conscience.[58]

The gendering of virtue, then, provided women with another vehicle by which they could move into the public realm, although this was not an immediate consequence. However, their emergence as novelists became the means to this end as it served to mediate the tension between the public and private spheres. This is the final point I wish to argue.

Public Versus Private and the Novel

The development of the novel both fostered and expanded the importance of personal relationships that characterized modern society. According to Watt, the novel reflected "the transition from the objective, social and public orientation of the classical world to the subjective, individualist and private orientation of the life and literature of the last two hundred years."[59]

In the course of its emergence the novel helped to create the concept of separate spheres, and its dominance as the modern narrative form by the nineteenth century enabled it to serve a mediatory function between the two realms. The novel made the private world the subject of public debate, and in so doing gave women an approved format to express their private thoughts regarding their publicly defined persona. Women not only had a vehicle with which to give voice to their own experience, but one that also allowed them to consider the significance of this experience in relationship to the wider society that formed the boundaries of this experience. "This conflict between public and private attitudes is one with which the novel in general has been much concerned, and which it is indeed peculiarly fitted to portray."[60]

As we have seen, the question of how narrative should connect public and private realms of experience is as old as the novel form itself. As one critic has noted, some novels "expose contradictions in the ideologies they use as well as the tensions in their narrative methods."[61] An apparent contradiction in ideologies is the tension between the Victorian notion of women's sphere and the growing influence of women as novelists.

Victorian society assumed that the public and private worlds were antithetical, hence their conception of masculinity and femininity were defined in opposition to each other. This is, in fact, the paradox of the Victorian world. The Christian values of truth, compassion, loyalty, and so on, were ensconced in the home, ever-guarded by the pure heart of the true woman. Her influence served as a reminder of these noble virtues to her husband and son who necessarily moved in a world where these values were continually at risk. Her capacity to develop and express these was dependent on her separation from the public world because only through separation could purity be maintained. And yet, the values of the private came increasingly to be seen as the solution to the ills of the public. The paradox that the Victorians sought to resolve was that society could be made similar to the family only if the family was isolated from society.[62]

When the public world was the center of moral authority, as in the aristocratic tradition, and men were the measure of the species, then only the stage on which they performed was definitive for the understanding of the meaning and purpose of human existence. However, with the shift in emphasis to the significance of private, individual actions as the arena in which moral contests were engaged, women's experience became a source of moral authority and instruction. While in its emergent form the novel contributed to the distinctions between the public and private realm, once it became established it also became the means by which these distinctions were dissolved. The novel purported to take the public into the private world of individual relationships, and in so doing made these relationships part of public discourse.

Armstrong argues that the apparently apolitical language of the novel in actuality served a distinct political end; as a form of moral expression, the novel was the vehicle destined to make public women's voice. I would go even further to suggest that this vehicle continues to be uniquely suited to women's expression as marginal members of society. I have already noted that critics, especially Armstrong and McKeon, understand the novel to be one of the primary agents in instituting the middle class. It then established itself as the literature of choice for this group. The early women novelists were overwhelmingly members of this class, and as such they shared the same values and attitudes.[63] In their subject matter, and in the construction of the moral dilemmas faced by their characters, women were not dramatically different from their male counterparts. By and large they accepted the dictum that women's true place was home and family. "As novelists, women have always been self-conscious, but only rarely self-defining."[64]

However, the emphasis on individualism in the modern novel meant that this was a community whose identity was rooted in the concept of discontinuity between its members and the authority of experience. This is not to say that Victorians celebrated rejection of common standards of behavior and thought; far from it. They still maintained the value of conformity, particularly for women. However, the emphasis on the individual recognized that individual interest could, and often did, come in conflict with social expectations, and that these conflicts could be a source of moral instruction. The assumption was no longer that conflict was, *prima facie*, a sign of moral failure (rebellion against received authority), but rather that in the resolution of conflict moral strength or weakness was revealed. It was in the process of resolution that value judgments lay.

The moral authority of women was dependent on their exclusion from the public world, yet as they entered into public moral debate as novelists, they reflected an increasing tension between public and private domain. In this sense, I believe, the novel continued to serve in a mediating capacity. Narrative expression had enabled the development of a new consciousness, relocating authority from tradition to experience, and the novel served to define the boundaries of the public and private realms. Similarly, in the nineteenth century, the novel continued to reconcile tensions arising from the shifting of those boundaries, resulting in changing concepts of the public/private construct.

The virulent attacks against women who sought to enter the closed male world of the university are only one expression of this tension, although attacks on women in general are perhaps the clearest indication of this since women were so strongly identified with the private world. Victorian identity rested firmly on the foundation of the separation of the public and the private. However, as previously clearly identified lines of demarcation began to melt, due in part to women's increasing public voice, it is not surprising that the reaction would focus on the most readily identifiable symbol of separation. The literary genre that helped to create and glorified the separate worlds of men and women proved to be the most effective tool for those who became the primary target of its attack.

As women emerged as authors, they increasingly demanded acceptance as individuals. Early critics of women's novels tended to treat all women writers as simply representative of the "Female Novelist," and their critiques depended largely on whether or not these women conformed to preconceived notions of acceptability. However, just as women writers strove to make their characters believable as real people so, too, they demanded that they be taken seriously as writers. Charlotte Brontë required of her critics that they judge her work not as representative of male or female authorship, but solely on her merits as a specific author, independent of her sex.[65]

As the modern narrative form, the novel is an effective tool for moral expression by a marginal group in society. It assumes both identity and conflict in its structure and is able to mediate between these. This has been the incongruity of women's experience. On the one hand they are entirely conversant with the dominant culture of patriarchal society. They have had not only to live in it, but have been required to—by virtue of their status as wives, daughters, and mothers—participate in the definitions it engendered. Women have been required to understand the world of men. And yet, women have also known that while this was a world they moved in, it was one in which they more often than not were assigned a secondary role.

Because the modern novel assumes that agreement is not normative, it provides for the expression of voices that are part of, and yet not identical with, the dominant ideology. The novel stresses the importance of individual experience even when it is at variance with prevailing ideologies. In the preceding chapter I noted that women were excluded from the discipline of theology and as a result of this exclusion found alternative methods for the expression of their moral voice. Although this may, in part, account for women's employment of the novel, we can now see that it is also due to the fact that narrative provided a methodological model that was more ideally suited to their particular place in society. As a result, women were able to make public a heretofore private voice and to bring the experience of women's lives to bear authoritatively on discussions of moral debate.

This is clearly evidenced in women's struggle for university education, particularly as this related to degrees in theology. Ben Perry has argued that the novel developed at a time when there was a disintegration of common ideals "save those which . . . [are] confined to small groups where the cultural values sanctioned by tradition or communal life can be fostered for a while."[66] The universities of England were such a group. Within this closed enclave assumptions of a common identity and the authority of tradition still existed. However, while the universities sought to maintain the status quo, they were facing attacks on many fronts. One such disruption would be the new claim for supremacy of the sciences over the classics. This is only another instance of what McKeon has called the epistemological crisis that England underwent. Such claims challenged the assumptions of the old guard and undermined the very foundations on which their self-identity rested.

The intrusion of women in the universities epitomized the changes that were occurring, not only within the structure and curriculum, but also in the ideology that had been its mainstay. I believe that the reason theology became the last bastion of resistance is that, perhaps more than any other discipline, it depended on the authority of a received tradition. Theology, in part, seeks to create (or recreate) the world in the image of divinity; for centuries the meaning and manner of this creation had been defined by men. One way to protect this sacred work was to define the boundaries that surrounded it in a way that excluded women. However, as the locus of truth shifted from tradition to experience, and as the novel became the new narrative paradigm for the expression of this, the emergence of women as novelists provided a double threat. The determination to keep women out of theology was, in fact, a last-ditch effort to retain the traditional grounding of authority.

The exclusion of women from theology did not, however, keep women from engaging in moral debate; they found a new paradigm within which to make their voices heard. We have seen that through the medium of the novel women were able to bring to bear their heretofore privatized experiences as a method of commenting on their society. In so doing they challenged, if only by inference, the prevailing ideologies regarding the reality of women's experience. Discussion of the nature and purpose of reality is always a moral argument. When we propose certain modes of being as appropriate or fitting to human nature, we establish them as moral values. Therefore, as women novelists reflected on their lives within the dominant society, they brought to the fore new possibilities for understanding the meaning of human existence.

> If writing is not figured into political history, then political power will continue to appear as if it resides exclusively in institutions that are largely governed by men, and the role played by women at various stages in the middle-class hegemony will remain unexamined for the political force that it was and still is today.[67]

There are many women who used the novel as a means of moral and theological expression. However, I wish to focus my discussion on the writings of Dorothy L. Sayers, who, in the early twentieth century, was able to employ the narrative method as a means for entering the public debates of men and to gain credibility as a moral thinker, even as a theologian, through this medium.

NOTES

1. Gerald Graff, *Literature Against Itself* (Chicago: The University of Chicago Press, 1979), 1.

2. The identification of these three authors with the rise of the novel is also noted by George Sampson, *The Concise Cambridge History of English Literature* (New York: The MacMillan Company, 1941), 455–509; and in the standard classroom text, M. H. Abrams, et al., *The Norton Anthology of English Literature*, 3rd ed. (New York: W. W. Norton & Company, Inc., 1974), 1698–99. See also Ernest A. Baker, *The History of the English Novel*, vol. 1 (New York: Barnes & Noble, Inc., 1957), 11.

3. Ian Watt, *The Rise of the Novel* (Berkeley: University of California Press, English Edition; London: Chatto and Windus Ltd., 1957), 9.

4. Ben Edwin Perry, *The Ancient Romances* (Berkeley: University of California Press, 1967), 25.

5. Watt, *Rise of the Novel*, 11.

6. Watt, *Rise of the Novel*, 31.

7. Watt, *Rise of the Novel*, 32.

8. Watt, *Rise of the Novel*, 48.

9. Watt, *Rise of the Novel*, 48.

10. Michael McKeon, *The Origins of the English Novel 1600–1740* (Baltimore: The Johns Hopkins University Press, 1987), 2–3.

11. McKeon, *Origins*, 3.

12. Nancy Armstrong, *Desire and Domestic Fiction: A Political History of the Novel* (New York: Oxford Univesity Press, 1987).

13. Armstrong, *Desire and Domestic Fiction*, 7.

14. Armstrong, *Desire and Domestic Fiction*, 8.

15. McKeon, *Origins*, 18.

16. McKeon, *Origins*, 19.

17. McKeon, *Origins*, 19.

18. McKeon, *Origins*, 20.

19. McKeon, *Origins*, 20.

20. McKeon, *Origins*, 20.

21. McKeon, *Origins*, 22.

22. For the complete discussion of questions of truth see McKeon, *Origins*, Part I, 25–128. To support and illustrate his claims about these epistemological transitions McKeon draws on a wide variety of sources from all over Western Europe, not only England.

23. McKeon, *Origins*, 118.

24. McKeon, *Origins*, 128.

25. Questions of virtue are addressed in McKeon, *Origins*, Part II, 131–270. This transition, too, is well-documented.

26. McKeon, *Origins*, Part II, 133.

27. McKeon, *Origins*, Part II, 151.

28. McKeon, *Origins*, Part II, 166–67.

29. McKeon, *Origins*, Part II, 173.

30. McKeon, *Origins*, Part II, 210–11.

31. McKeon, *Origins*, Part II, 212.

32. McKeon, *Origins*, Part II, 419.

33. Armstrong, *Desire and Domestic Fiction*, 8.

34. Armstrong, *Desire and Domestic Fiction*, 10.

35. Armstrong, *Desire and Domestic Fiction*, 11.

36. Armstrong, *Desire and Domestic Fiction*, 42.

37. McKeon, *Origins*, 255–65.

38. Watt, *Rise of the Novel*, 157.

39. Armstrong, *Desire and Domestic Fiction*, 49.

40. Armstrong, *Desire and Domestic Fiction*, 63.

41. Armstrong, *Desire and Domestic Fiction*, 66.

42. Armstrong, *Desire and Domestic Fiction*, 69.

43. Armstrong, *Desire and Domestic Fiction*, 118.

44. Armstrong, *Desire and Domestic Fiction*, 119.

45. Armstrong, *Desire and Domestic Fiction*, 253.

46. Perry, *Ancient Romances*, 63.

47. Watt, *Rise of the Novel*, 85.

48. Inga-Stina Ewbank, *Their Proper Sphere: A Study of The Brontë Sisters as Early-Victorian Female Novelists* (Cambridge, Mass.: Harvard University Press, 1966), xvi.

49. Margaret L. Anderson, *Thinking About Women: Sociological and Feminist Perspectives* (New York: Macmillan Publishing Co., 1984), 213.

50. Watt, *Rise of the Novel*, 43.

51. Elaine Showalter, *A Literature of Their Own* (Princeton, N.J.: Princeton University Press, 1977), 3.

52. Armstrong, *Desire and Domestic Fiction*, 255.

53. Samuel Pickering, *The Moral Tradition in English Fiction 1785–1850* (Hanover, N.H.: The University Press of New England, 1976), vii.

54. Ewbank, *Their Proper Sphere*, 23.

55. Ewbank, *Their Proper Sphere*, 41.

56. Patricia Meyer Spacks, *The Female Imagination* (New York: Alfred A. Knopf, 1975), 38.

57. Janet Horowitz Murray, "Introduction" in *Strong-Minded Women and Other Lost Voices from Nineteenth-Century England* (New York: Pantheon Books, 1982), 7.

58. Showalter, *Literature of Their Own*, 84.

59. Watt, *Rise of the Novel*, 176.

60. Watt, *Rise of the Novel*, 168.

61. Catherine Gallagher, *The Industrial Reformation of English Fiction: Social Discourse and Narrative Form 1832–1867* (Chicago: The University of Chicago Press, 1985), 184.

62. Gallagher, *Industrial Reformation*, 120.

63. Showalter, *Literature of Their Own*, 37.

64. Showalter, *Literature of Their Own*, 4.

65. Showalter, *Literature of Their Own*, 96.

66. Perry, *Ancient Romances*, 47.

67. Armstrong, *Desire and Domestic Fiction*, 256.

4

Dorothy Sayers: Novelist and Theologian

In the preceding chapters I have examined the different forces that contributed to the development of women's narrative voice as a form of moral argument. I now want to examine the work of one woman in particular, Dorothy L. Sayers. There are several reasons why Sayers provides a good subject of inquiry. Although both Oxford and Cambridge admitted women to university education in the late nineteenth century, it was not until 1920 that Oxford granted degrees to women for the first time. When this occurred, Sayers was among this group. Also, Dorothy Sayers first gained repute as a novelist, created the Lord Peter Wimsey detective stories. As Carolyn Heilbrun has noted, aside from Sherlock Holmes, Lord Peter was probably the most famous and best-loved detective in English fiction.[1] Finally, Sayers eventually went on to write theology, becoming a "formidable Christian apologist."[2]

Beyond these reasons, however, Sayers also had insight into her craft that I think has significant implications for an understanding of women's narratives as theological argument. Sayers argued that the creative work of the author was, in fact, an image of divine creativity. Therefore, her task as a novelist had theological implications, and she wrote extensively about what these might be. In Sayers, then, we have not only a woman who wrote both novels and theology, but also a woman who reflected on the meaning of her work, for her own life and as she extended it to life in general. "As she developed her craft, she discovered her vision and her voice. . . . Her popular art gave her a medium to express what she discerned in her society."[3]

I am not claiming that Dorothy Sayers was a feminist, although she had some insightful comments to make regarding women that I will deal with later. What I am arguing is that the way she understood herself as a woman novelist and theologian are significant for the development of a feminist methodology.

For those who are unfamiliar with Sayers's life, a brief biographical sketch might be helpful.[4] She was born, an only child, June 13, 1893, in Oxford, England. Her father was the headmaster of the Cathedral Choir School and had also served as chaplain of both Christ Church College and New College, Oxford. When she was about four her father took a country parish, and for the next twenty years the rectory was to be Sayers's home.

Her parents did not subscribe to the Victorian notions about a woman's "proper place" and from her youth Sayers was encouraged to develop her mind. At the age of seven her father undertook to teach her Latin, and by the age of thirteen she was also proficient in French and German. In 1909 she was sent to boarding school to continue her education, and she excelled scholastically, eventually winning the prestigious Gilchrist Scholarship in Modern Languages at Somerville College, Oxford. While at Oxford she was to develop the discipline that would thereafter mark her scholarship, and she graduated with honors in Trinity term, 1915 (although she did not receive her degree at this time).

During the next few years she undertook a variety of jobs, none of which seemed to satisfy her, and suffered the pangs of an unrequited love. In October of 1920, at the age of twenty-seven, she returned to Oxford to receive both her bachelor's and her master's degree at the first ceremony in which women were granted degrees. She then went to London, where she taught languages for a time, but in 1922 she took a job at Benson's advertising agency where she would work for the next nine years.

It was while she was at Benson's that she decided to try her hand at writing detective fiction, an idea she had been toying with for some time. Detective fiction was very popular at this time, and she thought it would be a good way to make some money. Her first novel, *Whose Body?*, which introduced the character of Lord Peter Wimsey, was published in 1923. From this point on her career as a writer was established, and she never looked back.

Shortly after the publication of *Whose Body?*, Sayers took a leave of absence from Benson's, ostensibly to complete another novel, but in reality she was pregnant. On January 3, 1924, she gave birth to a son who she named John Anthony. No name was recorded for the father on the birth certificate, and although there has been much speculation about who he might have been, it is relatively unimportant since he had no hand in raising her son. Although Sayers entrusted the care of her child to a cousin, she supported him financially and visited him when able.

In 1925 she met Oswald Atherton Fleming and married him the following year. Although he was handsome and dashing, he had been deeply disturbed by his experience in the war, and appears to have been a rather weak counterpart for this strong and dynamic woman. Nevertheless, they remained married until his death in 1950.

During the next nine years Sayers was to write all the rest of her Wimsey novels, in addition to editing other works of detective fiction and translating *The Romance of Tristan*. In 1937, however, she ended her work with Lord Peter. In that year she wrote *The Zeal of Thy House* in which she first began to clearly articulate her concept of creative work as divine image. A few years later she wrote *The Man Born to Be King,* a series of twelve radio plays on the life of Christ. She was also to write a considerable number of essays on diverse subjects, but increasingly dealing with theological themes. "To her reputation as a writer of detective fiction and of drama she added a new reputation as a spokesman [sic] for the church."[5]

In 1941 she wrote *The Mind of the Maker,* in which she expanded the ideas she had presented in *The Zeal of Thy House* on the creative and sacramental nature of work.

For the remainder of her life Dorothy Sayers continued to write extensively, publishing several collections of her essays, undertaking both critical work and translations of Dante, and also a translation of *The Song of Roland.* She died suddenly at her home on December 17, 1957.

Although this is only the briefest sketch of a rich and complex life, it should serve to provide some indication of the range and depth of this woman. I now want to consider three subjects that were important in the work and thought of Dorothy Sayers, and then go on to examine one of her novels, *Gaudy Night.* In this novel we have an excellent opportunity to observe the way in which Sayers employed narrative as a means of dealing with both moral and theological issues. In addition, we have the added benefit of her own reflections on this novel. Finally I will consider the implications of these themes for an application of feminist analysis. The three themes I will discuss are the creative mind as divine image, the integrity of work, and the humanity of women.

THE CREATIVE MIND AS DIVINE IMAGE

The Mind of The Maker represents the summation of Sayers's theological thought[6] and has been called her "most profoundly original book."[7] As one critic has noted, "Her goal was to . . . stir the soul, to awaken the imagination and the intellect . . . to get at what is most exciting about life itself, its creative vitality."[8] In this book she sought to explore and explain the nature of the human creative task and the implications this might have for an understanding of human work. "For her, the real adventure was the journey of the inquiring mind."[9]

Sayers was a Christian and therefore sought to understand the meaning of her life and work in relationship to Christian doctrine. Christian tradition teaches that human beings are created in the image of God, and Sayers addressed the question of how this might be so. Reflecting on her own work as a creative artist, Sayers came to the conclusion that human beings image God in "the desire and ability to make things."[10] However, Christian doctrine also maintains that God is a trinity, the divine Three-in-One. How are human beings to understand themselves, and their creative work, as reflecting this tripartite nature? Based on her understanding of the creative process, Sayers drew an analogy between this process and the trinitarian nature of God.

> . . . [T]he Trinitarian structure which can be shown to exist in the mind of man and in all his works is, in fact, the integral structure of the universe, and corresponds . . . by a necessary uniformity of substance, with the nature of God. . . ."[11]

She began with her own experience and then extrapolated from this in an attempt to reconcile the apparently disparate natures of humanity and the sacred. "It is this personal experience of the process of making that becomes for her an analogy of the Divine Mind. . . ."[12]

Human beings are created in the image of God in that we, too, create. Not that we create exactly as does God, who creates out of nothingness. But of all acts of human creation she believed that the artist perhaps comes closest to this experience. This is so because a work of art has a real existence apart from its translation into its material form; it exists in the mind of the maker. Without the prior thought the form cannot and does not exist. "This represents the nearest approach we experience to 'creation out of nothing' and we conceive of the act of absolute creation as being an act analagous to that of the creative artist."[13] As one critic has phrased it, for Dorothy Sayers "God is the archetype of the creator; the artist is a type."[14]

If, however, human beings image God in their creativity, and if God is a trinity, how does the creative task reflect this? Sayers is not the only Christian thinker to suggest that the doctrine of the trinity is perhaps the most mysterious of all Christian doctrines, and yet its centrality to the faith means that an account must be made of it. ". . . [T]he doctrine of the Trinity, if it is true, must be acceptable, even attractive, to devout intelligence and imagination. . . . But *what, in human thought or experience, can God the holy trinity be like?*"[15] However, as Sayers pointed out, with her usual common sense, there is nothing so mysterious in life that it does not correspond to something within human knowledge, and for her this was the experience of creating.[16]

This analogy is one she first set forth in the concluding speech of St. Michael in the play *The Zeal of Thy House.*

> For every work [*or act*] of creation is threefold, an earthly trinity to match the heavenly.
> First, [*not in time, but merely in order of enumeration*] there is the Creative Idea, passionless, timeless, beholding the whole work complete at once, the end in the beginning: and this is the image of the Father.
> Second, there is the Creative Energy [*or Activity*] begotten of that idea, working in time from the beginning to the end, with sweat and passion, being incarnate in the bonds of matter: and this is the image of the Word.
> Third, there is the Creative Power, the meaning of the work and its response in the lively soul: and this is the image of the indwelling Spirit.
> And these three are one, each equally in itself the whole work, whereof none can exist without the other: and this is the image of the Trinity.[17]

The Creative Idea, Creative Activity, and Creative Power thus reflect the Father, Son, and Spirit of the Holy Trinity, respectively. The most troublesome of these three, said Sayers, is the concept of the Creative Idea, because although the Idea precedes any mental or physical work on the story, the formulation of the Idea is its self-awareness in the Activity. "The writer cannot even be conscious of his Idea except by the working of the Energy which formulates it to himself."[18]

How, then, can one know that the Idea exists independently of the Activity? Because the Activity is brought into conformity with the Idea. In the same way Christian doctrine teaches that the Father was prior to the Son, and that the Son is the image of the Father. In this way the Activity "brings about an expression in temporal form of the eternal and immutable Idea."[19]

The Creative Power flows back to the writer from her own creative activity and is also the means by which the Activity is communicated to other readers, producing a corresponding response in them. From the perspective of the reader, the Power is the book.[20]

However, although each aspect has a reality of its own, all three are essentially inseparable. They are all present in the act of creation. "These things are not confined to the material manifestation: they exist in—they *are*—the creative mind itself."[21]

It is evident that Dorothy Sayers's theology is an experiential theology; she draws on her own experience as a creator to know how we might understand the creative nature of God. "This respect for experience . . . for reality, individually and particularly perceived, is central to Sayers' aesthetic and practice."[22] If human beings are indeed made in the image of God, then human reality must reflect this in some way, and it is not only appropriate, but unavoidable, to approach divinity from a human starting point. "To complain that man measures God by his own experience is a waste of time; man measures everything by his own experience; he has no other yardstick."[23] Sayers grounds her theology in her experience of making and builds from there.

The artist is one who images forth something. The creative mind works

> by building up new images, new intellectual concepts, new worlds. . . . Creation proceeds by the discovery of new conceptional relations between things, so as to form them into systems having a consistent wholeness corresponding to an image in the mind, and consequently, possessing real existence.[24]

The image expresses that which it images, just as the Son expresses the Father. But just as the Son is not inferior to the Father, so a work of art, which is an expression of an experience, is neither inferior to, or reducible to, that experience. The expression and the experience are one. "You only experience a thing when you can express it— however haltingly—to your own mind."[25]

The power of the creative artist is the power not only of expression, but the ability to express her experience in such a way that others may share in it. In the image of her experience, we recognize our own.[26]

THE INTEGRITY OF WORK

Dorothy Sayers's understanding of the significance of human work follows naturally from her understanding of her own work. As we can expect, she saw this as a Christian interpretation of the meaning of human work; it is a vocational approach to work.

She began with the assertion that human nature is expressed in our creative endeavors: ". . . man's fulfillment of his nature is to be found in the full expression of his divine creativeness. . . ."[27] If human beings are created in the image of God, then true humanity is realized in the way we most directly image divinity. Therefore, our work, understood correctly, is where we work out our humanity.

She divided humanity into two groups regarding their attitude toward work. The first, and largest group, has fallen prey to what she called the "economic fallacy" that work is only something that one does in order to get enough money to enable one to cease working.[28] For this group, work is a hateful necessity. The second group is much smaller, but happier. These are the people for whom work is an opportunity for enjoyment and self-fulfillment; their work and their life are one.[29]

Since she wanted to articulate a Christian theology of vocation, she felt it necessary to explain what she perceived as a Christian understanding of work. First of all she said "work is not, primarily, a thing one does to live, but the thing one lives to do."[30] One's work ought to provide for spiritual, mental, and bodily satisfaction. The primary reason for doing any job should not be the status that attaches to it or the income derived from it, but the fact that it is the job one *wants* to do. Every person should do the job to which he or she is best suited.

Secondly, "every maker and worker is called to serve God *in* his profession or trade—not outside it."[31] All human work, if it is the right job, is an opportunity to image the divine, and is therefore sacred. Finally, Sayers claimed that "the worker's first duty is to *serve the work*."[32] Too often individuals are persuaded to do a certain task because of the good it will do for society. However, any work that is done primarily to serve the community will never be well done. The only way to truly serve the community is to forget the community. If the worker is constantly concerned with pleasing others, her work will eventually end up doing no more than filling a public demand, and will therefore have no intrinsic integrity.

This view of work is obviously an idealistic one, and Sayers recognized the disparity between her ideal vision and the economic realities of the world in which she lived. She knew that necessity made it virtually impossible for more than a few persons to achieve this level of self-expression in their work. Remember, however, she is discussing what work *ought* to be if human beings are to image forth their true spiritual natures. Her comments, therefore, can be understood as a critique of her society, which maintained conditions that made work, for most people, a hateful necessity, and Sayers was outspoken in her criticism of these conditions.

THE HUMANITY OF WOMEN

Finally, I want to examine the comments of Dorothy Sayers in relationship to women. It has been said that she was not a feminist.[33] She was certainly hesitant to identify herself with what she called "the wrong kind of feminism."[34] And yet, in both her writings and her "uncompromising life" it is clear that neither did she side with anti-feminist factions.[35] She only addressed the subject of women directly on three occasions; in two essays entitled "Are Women Human?" and "The Human-Not-Quite-Human," and in her introduction to Dante's *Purgatory*. However, her comments are insightful and at times scathing, and lead us to understand that Dorothy Sayers did not subscribe to the notion of the inherent inferiority of the female sex.

To ask whether or not she was a feminist is perhaps not a fair question, for if we mean feminism as self-identification with a particular political platform, then it is clear that she did not align herself with any such group. "The liberation of women was not a cause she espoused, but a way of life she practiced on the premises that male and female are adjectives qualifying the noun 'human being,' and that the substantive governs the modifier."[36] Given this understanding, what did she have to say on the subject?

Sayers resisted what she called "aggressive feminism," by which she meant women imitating men's lives simply because they are men's lives.[37] When women take this position they run the risk of copying not only what is of value in men's lives, but also men's failings and absurdities.[38] It is ridiculous, she argued, to claim women are as good as men, unless one adds "at doing what?"[39]

For Dorothy Sayers, each human being is an individual and must be understood as such. She thought it repugnant for anyone to be viewed merely as representative of a particular class or group and not as an individual. Just as men laid claim to the identity of the individual, so did women have individual tastes, preferences, and ideas, and they wanted to be accepted on the basis of these. The problem was that men (and perhaps feminists) viewed women as a class. "What we ask is to be human individuals, however peculiar and unexpected."[40]

She extended this discussion to the realm of work and pointed out that women should be able to do whatever job they wanted to do. Women were often attacked when they moved into some heretofore domain of male privilege, and Sayers cautioned women against viewing men's jobs as desirable simply because they were men's jobs. "The only decent reason for tackling any job is that it is *your* job, and *you* want to do it."[41]

Just as men need meaningful work to do, so do women. However, the modern State had removed all women's useful domestic occupations and relocated them in the factory, insisting instead on her enforced idleness. Since no human being can be happy if not involved in a fulfilling work, men should not have been surprised that women were now demanding access to the male arena. Sayers pointed out that men had adopted the "sound principle" that the best qualified should do the job, but if that was to be effective, it must be a universal rule and apply to both men and women. "Once lay down the rule that the job comes first, and you throw that job open to every individual. . . ."[42]

One could argue, at this point, that Sayers did not address the deeper ontological issue of the presumed inherent inferiority of women. However, she commented on this in "The-Human-Not-Quite-Human," and her biting sarcasm made it clear what she thought of this concept: It is patently absurd.

The problem, she said, is that to the careless observer it appears that women are unlike men. However, they are more like men than they are like anything else: They are both human beings. "*Vir* is male and *Femina* is female: but *Homo* is male and female."[43] Unfortunately, men have persistently denied this. Although man is always dealt with as both *Vir* and *Homo,* woman is always, exclusively, *Femina.*

It was not only in this essay that she attacked "the male-made mythology of women."[44] Ralph Hone calls attention to her introduction to Dante's *Purgatory,* where "Sayers felt it incumbent upon her to contest vigorously the psychology-oriented criticism of Dante dominated by the 'mother-image.' "[45]

But it is very observable that whereas there has been from time immemorial an Enigma of Woman, there is no corresponding Enigma of Man. . . . The sentiment, "Man's love is of man's life a thing apart; 'tis woman's whole existence" is, in fact, a piece of male wishful thinking, which can only be made to come true by depriving the life of leisured woman of every other practical and intellectual interest. . . . The exaltation of virginity, the worship of the dark Eros, the apotheosis of motherhood, are alike the work of man. . . .[46]

If women react against men's definition of them, "he knows better, for she is not human, and may not give evidence on her own behalf."[47]

Dorothy Sayers suggested that if the tables were turned men might find that they fared no better than women. This perception of women was due, in large part, to the fact that a man did not take the trouble "to imagine how strange his life would appear to himself if it were unrelentingly assessed in terms of his maleness; if everything he wore, said, or did had to be justified by reference to female approval. . . ."[48]

In this essay she also related her discussion of women to the issue of work, and pointed out that, in fact, men have never complained when poor women have undertaken back-breaking and unsatisfactory labor. The reaction of men against women working only came as women began to compete for the interesting or exciting jobs. Men took the best work for themselves and demanded that women stay at home, dependent on men. Men labored and women exploited their labor. "And if the woman submits, she can be cursed for her exploitation; and if she rebels, she can be cursed for competing with the male: whatever she does will be wrong, and that is a great satisfaction."[49]

Dorothy Sayers pointed out that men continually ask what women want, as if it were the greatest mystery in the world. The reason they cannot seem to understand women is that, as far as men are concerned, women are not human and therefore could not possibly want the same things that men, who are human, want. Sayers obviously rejected this conception of the not-quite-human-human. What do women want?

> . . . [A]s human beings they want, my good men, exactly what you want yourselves: interesting occupation, reasonable freedom for their plea-sures, and a sufficient emotional outlet. . . . You know that this is so with yourselves—why will you not believe that it is so with us?[50]

The divine image of the creative mind, and the significance of work as the arena in which one works out one's humanity, were themes Sayers dealt with throughout her life. She understood these concepts on the basis of her own experience as a maker in love with her craft. But she was also a woman, and so it is fair to say that she understood her experience as a woman who was a creator. She always understood herself first as a human being, but this did not negate her womanhood, and she was therefore sensitive to restrictions placed on women in society that worked against women's humanity.

DOROTHY SAYERS AND DETECTIVE FICTION

I now want to look briefly at one of her novels in which all of these themes come together: *Gaudy Night*. This novel was the last true Lord

Peter detective story. She did write one more Wimsey novel, *Busman's Honeymoon,* but she subtitled this "A Love Story with Detective Interruptions."[51] She also began one other Wimsey tale, *Thrones, Dominations,* but this was never completed. As the last detective novel, then, *Gaudy Night* represents a culmination of her narrative work. "Of all her novels, *Gaudy Night* may alone be called the one toward which Sayers worked."[52] Sayers herself said the following about the novel: " 'By choosing a plot that should exhibit intellectual integrity as the one great permanent value in an emotionally unstable world I should be saying the thing that, in a confused way, I had been wanting to say all my life.' "[53] One of her critics has called it the "penultimate" Wimsey novel; ". . . a book that clearly marks a change in her attitude toward her responsibilities as a writer."[54]

If we keep in mind Sayers's understanding of the creative task we know that she did not write this merely for entertainment, or to please her reading public with another tale. She had something to say with her novels, and believed that of all her stories she said it best in this one. According to Sayers the overriding "Father-Idea" of this novel was integrity.[55] She not only deals with the issue of the integrity of work, but also integrity in human relationships.

A brief plot synopsis will provide a context for a discussion of these issues as related to the novel. The story actually centers not on Lord Peter, but on Harriet Vane, who Sayers had introduced as Wimsey's love interest in *Strong Poison.* In that novel Peter first encountered Harriet when she was being tried for the murder of her lover. He intuitively knows that she could not have committed the crime of which she was accused and sets about to secure her freedom, which he does, leaving her with a sense of being forever in his debt; of never being on equal footing with Peter. As a result, she rejects his proposal of marriage; any relationship must always begin with the presumption of equality. Harriet also appeared as a central character in another novel, *Have His Carcase,* in which she and Peter join forces to solve a murder mystery. In this story Peter renews his proposals of marriage, but Harriet continues in her rejection.

More than one biographer has commented on the similarities between Vane and Sayers. Both were Oxford scholars; both were disappointed in love affairs when young; both were successful writers of detective fiction; both were strong, nonconformist women. Although Sayers resisted attempts by her critics to identify her with any of her characters, there are enough similarities between these two women that the reader may assume that Sayers felt an affinity with Harriet

Vane. For this reason it is fair to understand Harriet's narrative as, in part, an expression of Sayers's voice.

Gaudy Night opens as Harriet receives an invitation from her college at Oxford, Shrewsbury, to attend their annual Gaudy, and with much hesitation she decides to go.[56] Her discomfort is due, of course, to all that has occurred in her life, and her anticipation of the reaction of the members of the university to the fact that she had been tried in an unsavory murder case. While at the Gaudy she receives an anonymous note, made up of letters cut from a newspaper, which calls her "a dirty murderess." She also finds a drawing that "depicted a naked figure of exaggeratedly feminine outlines, inflicting savage and humiliating outrage upon some person of indeterminate gender clad in a cap and gown."[57] After returning home she receives a second note that threatens both her and Peter.

Harriet assumes that these are all directed exclusively at her, but she soon hears from the Dean of Shrewsbury, who asks if she could come up to help them with a problem. It turns out that members of both the faculty and the student body have been receiving similar poison pen letters and obscene drawings, and that several destructive "pranks" have been played against the college. The most notable of these was the destruction of the proof sheets of a scholarly manuscript being prepared for publication by one of the faculty, Miss Lydgate.

Harriet agrees to help unravel the mystery, but it becomes more and more complex, and the attacks become increasingly vicious. Lord Peter finally arrives on the scene, and together they resolve the mystery. It seems that one of the women employed as a scout by the college, Annie, had once been married to a man named Arthur Robinson. He had been a scholar, and just as he was about to receive his M.A., a woman scholar, Miss de Vine, had discovered that he had suppressed evidence that would refute his thesis, and she exposed him. As a result, he lost his degree and his position. He eventually committed suicide and left his wife and children to fend for themselves.

Miss de Vine had come to Shrewsbury, and Annie had followed and secured a position there so that she could take revenge for what she perceived as the murder of her husband. In her twisted mind, not only was Miss de Vine guilty, but so were all women who took men's jobs away from them and who betrayed the true calling of womanhood (husband, home, and children), usurping men's position.

In the midst of all this detecting, Harriet and Peter also resolve the difficulties that had kept them apart, and the novel closes with them locked in an embrace.

As I said, one of the main themes of this book was the integrity of work, and it is presented as a confrontation of values. "Is professional integrity so important that its preservation must override every consideration of the emotional and material consequences?"[58] This is a question that runs throughout the story. On the one hand, the value of one's work is constantly affirmed. In the beginning of the story, when Harriet is plagued by doubts about being at the Gaudy, she suddenly remembers what her presence at Shrewsbury signifies. "They can't take this away, at any rate. Whatever I may have done since, this remains. Scholar; Master of Arts; Domina; Senior Member of this University . . . a place achieved, inalienable, worthy of reverence."[59] This same sense was reaffirmed to her later, during dinner, as the Warden proposed the toast of the university. "To be true to one's calling, whatever follies one might commit in one's emotional life, that was the way to spiritual peace."[60] At Sayers's own Somerville Gaudy in 1934 she was asked to propose the toast of the university, and this is likely a reflection of her own thoughts at that time.

Peter reiterates this same sentiment much later when he reflects, "If only one could root one's self in here among the grass and stones and do something worth doing, even if it was only restoring a lost breathing for the love of the job and nothing else."[61] However, the plot has been structured so that questions are raised about whether or not everything must be sacrificed to the integrity of the work. Peter pushes this question in an after-dinner discussion with the Senior members.

> "But does anybody here approve? A false statement is published and the man who could correct it lets it go, out of charitable considerations. Would anybody here do that? There's your test case, Miss Barton, with no personalities attached."
>
> "Of course one couldn't do that," said Miss Barton. "Not for ten wives and fifty children."
>
> "Not for Solomon and all his wives and concubines? I congratulate you, Miss Barton, on striking such a fine, unfeminine note. Will nobody say a word for the women and children? . . ."
>
> "You've got us in a cleft stick," said the Dean. "If we say it, you can point out that womanliness unfits us for learning; and if we don't, you can point out that learning makes us unwomanly."[62]

This is, of course, the context within which the issue of the integrity of one's work is raised. What is a woman's proper work? Is it motherhood, or may it as legitimately be scholarship? If the goal is to find the right work to do, then the wrong job, no matter how conscientiously one does it, will be done wrong. This question nags at Harriet throughout the novel. " 'Soured virginity'—'unnatural life'—'semi-demented spinsters'—'starved appetites and suppressed impulses'—'unwholesome atmosphere'—she could think of whole sets of epithets, ready-minted for circulation. Was this what lived in the tower set on the hill?"[63]

Annie obviously believed that this was an unnatural life for women.

> . . . [I]t seems to me a dreadful thing to see all these unmarried ladies living together. It isn't natural, is it? . . . [I]t seems a great shame to keep up this big place just for women to study books in. I can't see what girls want with books. Books won't teach them to be good wives.[64]

This may well have been an issue Sayers was attempting to resolve for herself in relationship to her own child. She obviously was not "mothering" him in a way that Annie (and many other women) would have thought appropriate. Sayers never brought her son to live in her home with Fleming, although he did take Fleming's name. "But he never became a significant part of her day-to-day life and was never legally adopted [by Fleming]."[65]

When Annie is finally discovered to be the villain, she is brought before her accusers and makes her final scathing attack.

> But couldn't you leave my man alone? He told a lie about somebody else who was dead and dust hundreds of years ago. Nobody was the worse for that. Was a dirty bit of paper more important than all our lives and happiness? You broke him and killed him—all for nothing. Do you think that's a woman's job? . . . A woman's job is to look after a husband and children. . . . I wish I could burn down this place and all the places like it—where you teach women to take men's jobs and rob them first and kill them afterwards.[66]

Against this background in which the integrity of work is measured against the emotional claims of human life, Harriet and Peter also work out their own relationship, and once again Sayers emphasized the concept of integrity. Harriet felt she could never come to Peter as an equal because she owed him too great a debt and because there was too great a disparity between their respective stations in life; Peter is, after all, a Lord. And yet, she is terribly attracted to him. In fact, she realizes one afternoon, with blinding clarity, that she loves him, but also knows that love in itself is not enough.

Early in the story Miss de Vine gives her the following advice:

> Detachment is a rare virtue, and very few people find it lovable, either in themselves or in others. If you ever find a person who likes you in spite

of it—still more, because of it—that liking has very great value, because it is perfectly sincere, and because, with that person, you will never need to be anything but sincere yourself.[67]

Throughout the story Harriet wrestles with the question of what it is about her that Peter loves, and what it is he wants from her in marriage. Her work is too important to her to give up, and yet she is afraid that is what marriage must entail. After all, the women faculty at Shrewsbury are single women, and too many of her ex-classmates have provided evidence that intellectual activity and marriage do not mix. "But," questions Harriet, "suppose one is cursed with both a heart and a brain?"[68]

She begins to understand Peter's perception of her when he does not presume to warn her away from what was becoming a dangerous pursuit.

> That was an admission of equality, and she had not expected it of him. If he conceived of marriage along those lines, then the whole problem would have to be reviewed in that new light; but that seemed scarcely possible. To take such a line and stick to it, he would have to be, not a man but a miracle.[69]

Of course, for those readers familiar with Peter Death Bredon Wimsey, he does quite often appear more miracle than man. He tells her that he loves her for her "devastating talent for keeping to the point and speaking the truth." Harriet reflects that "a more unattractive pair of qualities could seldom have been put forward as an excuse for devotion."[70] But it is Peter who tells the assembled women that "if it ever occurs to people to value the honor of the mind equally with the honor of the body, we shall get a social revolution of a quite unparalleled sort. . . ."[71]

The possibility that Peter might envisage marriage on these terms is one that Harriet wants to believe and yet is afraid to trust.

> Could there ever be any alliance between the intellect and the flesh? . . . Experience perhaps had a formula to get over this difficulty: one kept the bitter, tormenting brain on one side of the wall and the languorous sweet body on the other, and never let them meet. . . . But to seek to force incompatibles into a compromise was madness; one should neither do it nor be a party to it.[72]

Her fear is of losing herself in Peter, for, as she tells Miss de Vine, "If I once gave way to Peter, I should go up like straw." Yet, Miss de

Vine reminds her that Peter has never once taken advantage of that
fact. "You have had the luck to come up against a very unselfish and a
very honest man," Miss de Vine tells her. "You needn't be afraid of
losing your independence; he will always force it back on you. If you
ever find any kind of repose with him, it can only be the repose of a
very delicate balance."[73] That, in fact, is the repose Harriet eventually
finds with Peter. She finally accepts Peter's proposal not only, nor even
primarily, because he loves her, but because he values her work and
because his love springs from this respect.

To many of her readers, especially perhaps the women, there must
have been an exclamation of "At last!" Peter was, after all, a "catch"
by most standards. He was attractive, wealthy, intelligent, titled, and
sincerely in love with Harriet. "In having Harriet refuse the repeated
proposals of the wealthy and desirable Lord Peter, [Sayers] must have
shocked many in her audience."[74]

Harriet was well aware of Peter's desirability, but this is, in part,
what plagues her throughout the stories. Peter represented all that the
world respected and admired, and Harriet had broken with respecta-
bility in her life. She had a love affair but refused marriage, sacrificing
emotional security for intellectual integrity. She earned a comfortable
living, refusing to be dependent on a male provider, by writing murder
mysteries that many believed inappropriate to women's sensibilities.
But Harriet's middle name was Deborah, "the warrior-judge who is
the most unfeminine woman in the Old Testament."[75]

Harriet wrestled with the question of whether marrying a man
necessitated relinquishing her freedom of self-definition. She realized
that marriage to Peter was impossible until she had clearly established
her self, or she would lose herself in Peter. The site of their final
reconciliation is telling. It takes place at Oxford, and she and Peter are
both in full academic dress; both were members of the university. This
was not possible, however, until she had come to terms with her own
narrative.

Throughout the novel Sayers constantly interweaves these two
themes, integrity in one's work and integrity in one's relationships,
played out as a confrontation between the values of professional
integrity and the emotional consequences of this. She presents no easy
solutions. Although Peter and Harriet are able to resolve their differences, the larger issue represented through the character of Annie is
not easily solvable. Annie is apprehended, but her attacks on the
women scholars are not as neatly resolved; no final solution is offered.

As Sayers put it, "The only judgment this book can offer you is the book itself."[76]

Sayers commented on this difference between detective problems and the reality of life. Detective problems are completely solvable: The mystery was unraveled and Annie was apprehended. However, complete solutions are not always possible in life. Sayers exhibited that she was an artist in her craft in the creation and resolution of the detective problem. The difference, however, between detective stories and life is that life is not a problem to be solved.[77] In leaving this issue unresolved, Sayers allowed the reader to wrestle with it for herself, and to come to find her own answer to the questions that were posed.

I want to make one final observation about this novel. Although Sayers said that the main theme of the book was integrity, it is fair to ask why she set it within the plot structure she did. She could just as easily have constructed a story that would have dealt with the same theme outside the framework of the life of academic women. That she placed it within this sphere indicates that she wanted to comment on this idea also. Obviously, there were still many people in society who believed, as Annie did, that women had no place in academia, or any other male preserve. When this book was published in 1935, Cambridge was still not granting degrees to women. Sayers was not one of these; she herself was a scholar. Although she allows the character of Harriet Vane to have doubts about her life, and the lives of the women at Shrewsbury, it is clear that in her mind the resolution of these does not lie in the denial of academic life. Sayers believed that few women would usually find a job preferable to a home and family, and thought it regrettable that this was the choice women must usually make; either home or job. Men, by and large, did not have to make that choice. "He gets both. In fact, if he wants the home and the family, he usually has to take the job as well, if he can get it."[78]

We get some insight into her reasons behind this plot in her original concept of the book.

. . . Miss Sayers tells us, she was thinking of writing a "straight novel" about "an Oxford woman graduate who found, in middle life, and after a reasonably satisfactory experience of marriage and motherhood, that her real vocation and full emotional fulfillment were to be found in the creative life of the intellect."[79]

Although she eventually wrote *Gaudy Night* as another of the Wimsey stories, it is obvious that she also wanted to comment on the justifiability of women choosing a vocation other than, or in addition to, motherhood.

This, too, is a theme that runs throughout the novel. Early in the book Miss Hillyard, one of the Shrewsbury faculty, observes:

> All the men have been amazingly kind and sympathetic about the Women's Colleges. Certainly. But you won't find them appointing women to big University posts. . . . The women might perform their work in a way beyond criticism. But they are quite pleased to see us playing with our little toys.[80]

There is also the following conversation, which takes place between Lord Peter and the Shrewsbury Warden.

> The Warden supplied him with a little local history, breaking off to say:
>   "But probably you are not specially interested in all this question of women's education."
>   "Is it still a question? It ought not be. I hope you are not going to ask me whether I approve of women's doing this and that."
>   "Why not?"
>   "You should not imply that I have any right either to approve or disapprove."
>   "I assure you," said the Warden, "that even in Oxford we still encounter a certain number of people who maintain their right to disapprove."
>   "And I had hoped I was returning to civilization."[81]

The entire novel, of course, implies that in this case, Peter speaks for Sayers. It is not the academic women who are the villains. In fact, the true villain of the story is the deceased Arthur Robinson who, due to his lack of integrity in his work, occasions all the sad events that follow, including his failure in his relationship as husband and father. In this novel, then, Sayers makes clear her thoughts about the significance of human work, the inherent humanity of women, and the necessity for the recognition of these as factors in both men's and women's lives if there are to be relationships of equals. Having articulated these themes in her novel, she then put aside the narrative form and went on to write more specific theology.

> I know it is no accident that *Gaudy Night* . . . should be a manifestation of precisely the same theme as the play *The Zeal of Thy House,* which followed it and was the first of a series of creatures embodying a Christian theology.[82]

SAYERS AND WOMEN'S NARRATIVE VOICE

I have suggested that Dorothy Sayers's understanding of the creative mind, and the value of human work, are significant for a feminist understanding of women's narrative voice. As one critic has noted, given Sayers's conception of the creative endeavor "it is possible to view literature as religious in the profoundest sense . . . to understand it as exhibiting and communicating an experience that is analogous to the divine."[83] For Sayers, the true creative artist never wrote simply to provide entertainment, or even to provide moral instruction. As far as she was concerned, work that was undertaken for either of these reasons was no more than "pseudo art." This is not to say that good art might not entertain, and as is evidenced by her own work it very well might raise moral issues for consideration, but this should not be the motivation behind the creation. True art, in the image of the divine, must always be compelled by the joy of creation for its own sake.[84]

Although Dorothy Sayers left narrative to write more specifically theological material, the case can be made that her novels enabled her theology. The credibility and popularity she gained as a writer and a thinker through the Wimsey stories led her to write the play *Busman's Honeymoon.* The success of this play occasioned the invitation she received to write a play for the 1937 Canterbury Festival, for which she produced *The Zeal of Thy House.* It was in this play that she first began to expand her ideas on the creative nature of work, which led, of course, to *The Mind of the Maker.* Her theology, therefore, began with her narratives.

Sayers presented an analogy by which we might understand the spiritual nature of human creativity; she then left it up to each individual to understand how, and if, that analogy might be made intelligible in each person's own life. She was not prescriptive. "Critics are then free to relate it to whatever works their own imaginations can discover or . . . to render a fuller and more complete account of the creative act itself."[85] I now wish to exercise this freedom to suggest some ways in which her work might give a clearer understanding of the theological significance of women's narrative voice.

If Sayers is correct that in our creative work we image forth the divine, then by the very act of writing novels women have laid claim to the divine nature. "It should be remembered that creation and re-creation is the profoundest theme that runs throughout the whole Bible."[86] In the first two chapters I discussed the fact that women had been viewed primarily as procreators; the task of creation was one that belonged to men. In this, they claimed exclusivity to the divine image. As God created, so did men, and in this task they reserved the right to define what it meant to be human. "In making symbols, creating languages and symbolic systems, *Homo sapiens* becomes truly human."[87] Since women did not (were not permitted to) create, they were not beings in the image of God. As Sayers has pointed out, when women are denied access to creativity, we do "violence to the very structure of our being."[88]

In the power of creation, the creative artist brings something new into being. Sayers made it clear that creativity is not simply a rejection of what has gone before; creativity does not depend on originality of substance. It is the ability to bring a new vision of existent conceptions, and to do so in a way that they become authentic for others. I see this as analogous to McKeon's assertion that the novel is able to serve a mediatory function in its development. The author re-visions reality, and in so doing helps to image forth a new reality. Nancy Armstrong has shown that when women began to write they were engaged in both the process and product of a new location of moral authority.

Sayers maintained that the creative artist goes beyond the limits imposed by the definitions of reality she has received. In the process of re-visioning she addresses the "universal statement which forms its major premise."[89] This is a disturbing influence, because the definitions depend on the acceptance of the universal statement. When this is called into question, so are all attendant conceptions. The universal statement women challenged when they began to write was the premise of male exclusivity of creation, and this could not help but change the way in which reality was understood. "The hand of the creative artist, laid upon the major premise, rocks the foundations of the world. . . ."[90]

It is quite evident that Dorothy Sayers's theology is an experiential theology. It is based on her experience as a maker, which she claims is a valid way to understand God. In making such a claim for herself, she opens the door for other women to make similar claims about their own experience. What is important to note is the emphasis she places on the experience of the individual; the fact that it is not the experience of every human being does not invalidate it. She hopes that her experience will have meaning for others, however, "it is not her intention to exclude other people's experience, but wisely, to talk about the experience which she herself has had."[91] Her experience is as a novelist, and this has particular significance for her understanding of God.

Although all creative work is a divine image, there is a particular affinity between the work of the writer and the work of God. Christian theology teaches that when God created it was through the power of the word. "And God *said,* 'Let there be light'; and there was light" (Genesis 3:1, emphasis mine). The penultimate example of God is described as the Word made flesh. The author also creates through the power of the word. "For the artist, as for God, the tools of creativity are words."[92]

The power of the word is, says Sayers, a dangerous power, because the nature of the word is to incarnate itself. "It may for some time incarnate itself only in more words, more books, more speeches; but the day comes when it incarnates itself in actions, and this is its day of judgment."[93] As both Michael McKeon and Nancy Armstrong have made clear, the significance of the novel was to be found not only in its ability to reflect a changing society, but also to effect the movements that would bring about this change. It not only served as a vehicle for the incarnating of the middle class, but also aided the relocating of the ground of truth to the individual as conceived by the modern mind. The transition it helped to accomplish then provided the foundation on which Sayers would construct her theology, a theology extrapolated from the life experience of an individual woman.

Virginia Woolf argued that when women began to write it was a moment of great historical import. Nancy Armstrong asserted that, in *Pamela,* the idea that a young serving woman could claim authority over her own body was also a significant development in literature. Similarly, I think that when a woman novelist could declare that her personal life experience was an appropriate analogy for understanding the nature of God, and have that statement taken seriously, this is a notable event. It was only about seventy-five years before that John Ruskin had reminded women of the "nothingness of the proportion" that a woman's little world bore to the world of God. Now Sayers maintained that in her life and her work was the reflection of divine power, and that she, as a woman, had the right to exercise it.

Creative work empowers not only the author, but also her audience. For the author, the act of creating is one in which she gains control of her own experience.

> By thus recognising it in its expression, she makes it her own—integrates it into herself. She no longer feels herself battered passively by the impact of external events—it is no longer something happening *to* her, but something happening *in* her, the reality of the event is communicated to her in activity and power.[94]

If Sayers was using *Gaudy Night,* particularly the character of Harriet Vane, to resolve some of her own questions about the claims of personal relationships over and against the value of one's work (and I think she was), then it seems clear that this novel functioned in the manner described above.

For women, the process of writing is a process of self-definition. Nancy Armstrong has chronicled the development of the novel as the creation of a new paradigm in which moral authority came to be vested in the experience of women. Although in the early novels this authority was dependent of women's seclusion in the domestic household, I have suggested that the emergence of women as novelists began the transition of women to the public world by making their private voices part of the public domain. However, in this incarnation, their voices carried authority that they had not previously asserted, and because of this new authoritative voice, women began to create a different reality in which the weight of their moral argument was brought to bear on the sphere from which they were excluded. In *Gaudy Night,* Sayers presented a critique of the academic system, which either excluded women or treated them as poor relations. She also suggested that women who chose a vocation other than wife and mother were not necessarily disappointed and embittered spinsters.

The woman author, therefore, is not only able to change her own reality by taking control of it, but is also able to re-vision reality for those who read her work; especially for other women. Because she is a woman like other women, at some level her experience will be common to all women. In the image of her experience we can recognize our own. "The personal *is* political." This is the creative power of the author. In the expression of the creative artist we can "recognize something that had happened to us, but which we had never understood, never formulated or expressed to ourselves, and therefore never known as real experience."[95] The author is a creator in that she creates a reality that has a new validity for having been written. Her reader then "can possess and take hold of it and make it [her] own, and turn it into a source of knowledge and strength."[96] The author enables and empowers other women to then create within their own lives; to re-vision their own experience.

Each person, each woman, said Sayers, needs meaningful work in order to be truly human. Only the individual knows what that work might be for her. But whatever it is, it must be the work that one finds joy in doing. Sayers sought to counteract what she perceived as the Puritan ethic that the highest work one does is work done out of duty to God and society. That kind of work is not pleasing to God, and is not the work in which we find our own image of divinity. The true merit in any work is the enjoyment one finds in the work itself.

Recall her caution that the first duty to one's work is to the work itself. All too often women's lives have been restricted on the basis that women always have a higher calling or duty—motherhood. Although a woman may wish to create other things with her life, this was to be her first obligation. Christian theology has, by and large, maintained that women's meaning and purpose in life is to be found in motherhood, and society has enjoined women to fulfill their duty to the State. However, that should be one's work only if it is the work one takes joy in doing, according to Sayers. If it is not, it will always be the wrong work. No matter how conscientiously one approaches it, it will never be work in which the divine is imaged forth. The sacred human experience is found in the outpouring of creativity, and there is no creative act in a job done out of duty.

Women (and also, at times, men) have been encouraged to deny the self in order to benefit the community; the community has often been held to come before personal interests or aspirations. The difference between this demand as it has been made on men and women is that the community we are enjoined to sacrifice ourselves to is one that women had little hand in defining. As a result women's good, their work, is subsumed so that the good of others (men) may be realized. This is unacceptable. ". . . [I]f we conclude that creative mind is in fact the very grain of the spiritual universe . . . we shall have to ask ourselves whether the same pattern is . . . exhibited in the spiritual structure of every man and woman."[97] If this is the case, then both men and women must have full opportunity to express this.

Harriet Vane maintained that the way to spiritual peace was to be true to one's calling. One's work, therefore, cannot be separated from one's spiritual nature, and the denial of one's work is a sacrilege. As women took up the pen, and began the process of re-visioning their world, as they laid claim to creative privilege, they began to chip away at the foundation of male authority, both social and theological.

The act of women writing makes a theological claim to full humanity and the right to define the sacred in the light of women's experience. Understood in this way, when women began to write they usurped the most closely guarded privilege of men: the authority to define humanity.

Women are not human. They lie when they say they have . . . interest directed immediately to God and His universe, not intermediately through any child of man. . . . They have feminine minds and feminine natures, but their mind is not one with their nature like the minds of men; they have no human mind and no human nature.[98]

Thus, comments Sayers, did men define women. As women write their own experience they deny this definition and take unto themselves the power of self-creation. Men may listen if they choose, but the power of the word has overthrown the authority of patriarchal definitions. Women create, and in so doing they image forth the divine in the aspect of the feminine.

NOTES

1. Carolyn Heilbrun, "Sayers, Lord Peter and God," in *Lord Peter: A Collection of All the Lord Peter Wimsey Stories*, ed. James Sandoe (New York: Harper & Row, Publishers, 1972), 454.

2. Heilbrun, "Sayers, Lord Peter and God," 454.

3. Dawson Gaillard, *Dorothy L. Sayers* (New York: Frederick Ungar Publishing Co., 1981), 1.

4. There are many biographies of Sayers available; the following list of titles is by no means exhaustive. James Brabazon, *Dorothy L. Sayers* (New York: Charles Scribner's Sons, 1981); Alzina Stone Dale, *The Story of Dorothy L. Sayers* (Grand Rapids, Mich.: William B. Eerdmans Publishing Company, 1978); Janet Hitchman, *Such a Strange Lady* (New York: Harper & Row, Publishers, 1975); Ralph E. Hone, *Dorothy L. Sayers: A Literary Biography* (Kent, Ohio: The Kent State University Press, 1979); Nancy M. Tischler, *Dorothy L. Sayers: A Pilgrim Soul* (Atlanta: John Knox Press, 1980).

5. Hone, *Dorothy L. Sayers*, 118.

6. Rosamond Kent Sprague, ed., *A Matter of Eternity: Selections from the Writings of Dorothy L. Sayers* (Grand Rapids, Mich.: William B. Eerdmans Publishing Company, 1973), 14.

7. Robert Paul Dunn, " 'The Laughter of the Universe': Dorothy L. Sayers and the Whimsical Vision," in *As Her Whimsey Took Her: Critical Essays on the Work of Dorothy L. Sayers*, ed. Margaret P. Hannay (Kent, Ohio: The Kent State University Press, 1979), 201.

8. Gaillard, *Dorothy L. Sayers*, 5.

9. Tischler, *Dorothy L. Sayers*, 2.

10. Dorothy L. Sayers, *The Mind of the Maker* (New York: Harcourt, Brace and Company, 1941), 22.

11. Sayers, *Mind of the Maker*, xiii.

12. Richard T. Webster, "*The Mind of the Maker*: Logical Construction, Creative Choice and the Trinity," in *As Her Whimsey Took Her: Critical*

Essays on the Work of Dorothy L. Sayers, ed. Margaret P. Hannay (Kent, Ohio: The Kent State University Press, 1979), 166.

13. Sayers, *Mind of the Maker*, 29.

14. Nancy Tischler, "Artist, Artifact, and Audience: The Aesthetics and Practice of Dorothy Sayers," in *As Her Whimsey Took Her: Critical Essays on the Work of Dorothy L. Sayers*, ed. Margaret P. Hannay (Kent, Ohio: The Kent State University Press, 1979), 153.

15. John Thurmer, *A Detection of the Trinity* (Exeter, England: The Paternoster Press, 1984), 11.

16. Sayers, *Mind of the Maker*, 35.

17. Sayers, *Mind of the Maker*, 37.

18. Sayers, *Mind of the Maker*, 39.

19. Sayers, *Mind of the Maker*, 40.

20. Sayers, *Mind of the Maker*, 41.

21. Sayers, *Mind of the Maker*, 41.

22. Tischler, "Artist, Artifact and Audience," in Hannay, *Critical Essays*, 155.

23. Sayers, *Mind of the Maker*, 24.

24. Dorothy L. Sayers, "Creative Mind," in Dorothy L. Sayers, *Unpopular Opinions* (New York: Harcourt, Brace and Company, 1947), 55.

25. Dorothy L. Sayers, "Toward A Christian Aesthetic," in Dorothy L. Sayers, *Unpopular Opinions* (New York: Harcourt, Brace and Company, 1947), 41–2.

26. Sayers, "Toward a Christian Aesthetic," 42.

27. Dorothy L. Sayers, "Creed or Chaos?", in Dorothy L. Sayers, *Creed or Chaos?* (New York: Harcourt, Brace and Company, 1949), 44.

28. Sayers, "Creed or Chaos?", 43.

29. Dorothy L. Sayers, "Living To Work," in Dorothy L. Sayers, *Unpopular Opinions* (New York: Harcourt, Brace and Company, 1947), 150.

30. Dorothy L. Sayers, "Why Work?", in Dorothy L. Sayers, *Creed or Chaos?* (New York: Harcourt, Brace and Company, 1949), 53.

31. Sayers, *Creed or Chaos?*, 57.

32. Sayers, *Creed or Chaos?*, 59.

33. Mary McDermott Shideler, "Introduction," in Dorothy L. Sayers, *Are Women Human?* (Grand Rapids, Mich.: William B. Eerdmans Publishing Company, 1971), 7; Tischler, *Dorothy L. Sayers*, 16.

34. Dorothy L. Sayers, "Are Women Human?", in Dorothy L. Sayers, *Are Women Human?* (Grand Rapids, Mich.: William B. Eerdmans Publishing Company, 1971), 22.

35. Tischler, *Dorothy L. Sayers*, 2.

36. Shideler, "Introduction," in Sayers, *Are Women Human?*, 7.

37. Sayers, "Are Women Human?", in Sayers, *Are Women Human?*, 17.

38. Sayers, "Are Women Human?", 21.

39. Sayers, "Are Women Human?", 18.

40. Sayers, "Are Women Human?", 29.

41. Sayers, "Are Women Human?", 23.

42. Sayers, "Are Women Human?", 25.

43. Dorothy L. Sayers, "The Human-Not-Quite-Human," in Dorothy L. Sayers, *Are Women Human?* (Grand Rapids, Mich.: William B. Eerdmans Publishing Company, 1971), 37.

44. Hone, *Dorothy L. Sayers*, 158.

45. Hone, *Dorothy L. Sayers*, 158.

46. Dorothy Sayers, "Introduction," in Dante Alighieri, The Florentine, *The Comedy of Dante Alighieri*, Cantica II, *Purgatory* (*Il Purgatorio*), trans. Dorothy L. Sayers (New York: Basic Books, Inc., Publishers, n.d.), 33.

47. Sayers, "The Human-Not-Quite-Human," in Sayers, *Are Women Human?*, 39.

48. Sayers, "The Human-Not-Quite-Human," 39.

49. Sayers, "The Human-Not-Quite-Human," 43–44.

50. Sayers, "Are Women Human?", in Sayers, *Are Women Human?*, 32.

51. This was originally created as a play in 1936, and was published as a novel in June, 1937.

52. Hone, *Dorothy L. Sayers*, 74.

53. Sayers, quoted in Gaillard, *Dorothy L. Sayers*, 72.

54. Dunn, "Laughter of the Universe," in Hannay, *Critical Essays*, 204.

55. Sayers, *Mind of the Maker*, 191.

56. I am compelled to comment on the name Sayers assigned to her fictional college. Sayers was a mistress of the English language and chose her words with great precision. Therefore, it is safe to assume that this name was not chosen simply by whim. I call the reader's attention to Mary Daly's definition of Shrew: "an Untamed and Untamable Turbulent Termagant," Mary Daly, in cahoots with Jane Caputi, *Websters' First New Intergalactic Wickedary of the English Language* (Boston: Beacon Press, 1987), 162. I think Sayers might have approved.

57. Dorothy L. Sayers, *Gaudy Night* (New York: Avon Books, 1968, Harper & Row Publishers Inc., 1936), 36.

58. Sayers, *Mind of the Maker*, 190.

59. Sayers, *Gaudy Night*, 13.

60. Sayers, *Gaudy Night*, 13, 28.

61. Sayers, *Gaudy Night*, 236.

62. Sayers, *Gaudy Night*, 287–88.

63. Sayers, *Gaudy Night*, 66.

64. Sayers, *Gaudy Night*, 102–103.

65. Tischler, *Dorothy L. Sayers*, 76.

66. Tischler, *Dorothy L. Sayers*, 372.

67. Tischler, *Dorothy L. Sayers*, 34–35.

68. Tischler, *Dorothy L. Sayers*, 149.

69. Tischler, *Dorothy L. Sayers*, 184.

70. Tischler, *Dorothy L. Sayers*, 280–81.

71. Tischler, *Dorothy L. Sayers*, 290.

72. Tischler, *Dorothy L. Sayers*, 350.

73. Tischler, *Dorothy L. Sayers*, 375–76.

74. Tischler, *Dorothy L. Sayers*, 83.

75. Tischler, *Dorothy L. Sayers*, 83.

76. Sayers, *Mind of the Maker*, 190.

77. Sayers, *Mind of the Maker*, 197–204.

78. Sayers, "Are Women Human?", in Sayers, *Are Women Human?*, 26.

79. Heilbrun, *Sayers, Lord Peter and God*, 465.

80. Sayers, *Gaudy Night*, 49.

81. Sayers, *Gaudy Night*, 276.

82. Sayers, *Mind of the Maker*, 207.

83. Richard L. Harp, "*The Mind of the Maker*: The Theological Aesthetic of Dorothy Sayers and Its Application to Poetry," in *As Her Whimsey Took Her: Critical Essays on the Work of Dorothy L. Sayers*, ed. Margaret P. Hannay (Kent, Ohio: Kent State University Press, 1979), 186.

84. Sayers, "Christian Aesthetic," in Sayers, *Unpopular Opinions*, 44–46.

85. Harp, "*Mind of the Maker*", in Hannay, *Critical Essays*, 199.

86. Harp, "*Mind of the Maker*," 178.

87. Gerda Lerner, *The Creation of Patriarchy* (New York: Oxford University Press, 1986), 199.

88. Sayers, *The Mind of the Maker*, 185. Although Sayers was referring to all human beings, male and female, when she made this statement, in this section of the chapter I am going to apply her comments specifically to the issue of women as creators, and therefore will use the feminine form even when she uses the term "man" in a generic way. I take the liberty to do so because Sayers has made it clear that she understood both men and women as equally human, and that she did not use the generic to imply the exclusion of women. Since I am dealing particularly with women, reading her comments in this light allows for greater coherency.

89. Sayers, *Mind of the Maker*, 211.

90. Sayers, *Mind of the Maker*, 212.

91. Webster, "*Mind of the Maker*," in Hannay, *Critical Essays*, 173.

92. Tischler, "Artist, Artifact and Audience," in Hannay, *Critical Essays*, 158.

93. Sayers, *Mind of the Maker*, 111.

94. Sayers, "Christian Aesthetic," in Sayers, *Unpopular Opinions*, 42.

95. Sayers, "Christian Aesthetic," 43.

96. Sayers, "Christian Aesthetic," 43.

97. Sayers, *Mind of the Maker*, 185.

98. Sayers, "The Human-Not-Quite-Human," in Sayers, *Are Women Human?*, 46.

5

Women's Novels and Narrative Theology

I have suggested that the emergence of women as novelists was the result of several diverse factors that culminated in the nineteenth century: the cultural and social assumptions regarding woman's nature, the changing structure and curriculum in the universities of Oxford and Cambridge, and finally the capacity of the novel to mediate epistemological and social transitions. I have further suggested that as women developed a narrative voice they understood their creative task as more than simply entertainment or representation; their writing also constituted their participation in public moral debate. In particular I have examined the work of Dorothy Sayers as an example of the way in which a woman's novelistic expression could also be understood as theological claim-making.

This is an argument I now wish to further consider. In what way were (and are) women's narratives representative of both public moral argument and theology, and how can they be located in contemporary discussions regarding narrative theology? The assertion that women's novels constitute a narrative theology is important both descriptively and prescriptively. On the one hand it can be argued that women are now moving into traditional forms of moral discussion as theologians, philosophers, ethicists, social scientists, and so on. Names such as Rosemary Ruether, Mary Daly, Beverly Harrison, Sharon Welch, and Carol Gilligan all come immediately to mind. Therefore, we might conclude that since these fields are opening to women, narrative will play a less important part in women's moral expression. However, I have maintained that narrative is a particularly effective tool for

marginal groups within society, and though women are moving into
the mainstream, their place is yet neither central nor assured.

In addition, we cannot ignore that women's stories are part of
women's history and are the process by which women are establishing
a tradition of women's experience. "Memory is the vessel which
retains in the present the record of the experiences undergone in the
past and of knowledge gained through the recorded and remembered
experiences of others, living and dead."[1] The individual's concept of
self is dependent, in part, on his or her memories. Women's stories
function to provide a shared memory by which we can understand
ourselves. The significance of this for women is clearly articulated by
Gerda Lerner.

> Women have for millennia participated in the process of their own
> subordination because they have been psychologically shaped so as to
> internalize the idea of their own inferiority. The unawareness of their own
> history of struggle and achievement has been one of the major means of
> keeping women subordinate.[2]

Women's stories provide one of the primary means for creating an
awareness of our history. The question that needs to be addressed is
what hold does our history, as revealed through stories, have on
contemporary women? What claim does it make on our lives?

Finally, in this chapter I will attempt to address a larger question in
relation to narrative theology. What are the assumptions of narrative
theologians regarding the meaning and purpose of stories? How do
they understand narrative to function, and what do these assumptions
suggest for a feminist methodology of narrative interpretation?

WHY STORIES?

The basic question from which we must proceed is whether or not
women's novels constitute a theological ground. Contemporary discussions regarding narrative theology suggest that they do. All the theorists agree that, in fact, narrative is antecedent to theology, or any
other kind of moral argument for that matter. The reason for this is
that all theologies presuppose a narrative—a story—against which
individual persons examine their lives. Stanley Hauerwas has stated
that "Every social ethic involves a narrative;"[3] Walter Fisher has
amended this to read "Any ethic, whether social, political, legal or

otherwise, involves narrative."[4] Edward Shils makes the assertion that "Every human action and belief has a career behind it. . . ."[5] According to Alasdair MacIntyre, "I can only answer the question 'What am I to do?' if I can answer the prior question 'Of what story or stories do I find myself a part?' "[6] Michael Goldberg reiterates this claim when he asserts that "propositional" theology always derives from a narrative.[7] All of these writers reflect an awareness that our lives are not devoid of context. If we proceed without acknowledging that context, we create distorted images of what it means to be in the world.

In addition, they all agree it is our stories that provide continuity in our lives and create the possibility of social existence.

> A society to exist at all must be incessantly reenacted, its communications must repeatedly be resaid . . . guided by what the individual members remember about what they themselves said and did before, what they perceive and remember of what other persons expect and require of them . . . by what they remember is expected and required of them. . . .[8]

We are able to act as a society because we have a common tradition that provides us with an overarching sense of what it means to be a member of the society. This is akin to Goldberg's understanding of the function of "paradigmatic stories," which he describes "as the background contexts in and against which our moral and religious convictions gain their meaning and significance. . . ."[9] Whatever community we belong to is defined by such stories (i.e., Jewish, Christian, American, etc.), and they provide a framework in which to examine our lives and understand how we are members.

Based on this shared understanding of the importance of stories, I want to consider women's stories in light of the concept of a narrative tradition. If it is true that we are storied people, that we discover the meaning of our lives in our narratives, then for women's lives to become truly authentic they need to first create their own narrative history. One might respond that women already share in existent narrative traditions, whether those be particular religious traditions (Christianity, Judaism, etc.), or simply the tradition we call Western culture.

However, I would maintain that *the* narrative tradition of Western civilization has been patriarchy.[10] All other paradigmatic narratives have developed under this umbrella. In fact, it is fair to say that our cultural tradition is a masculine autobiography. This is not because women were not a part of it, but because until very recently they did not participate in the framing of the narratives.

In discussing tradition Edward Shils has identified two concepts of the past. The first he calls the "sequence of occurred events." "This is the real past which has happened and left its residues behind . . . [the] hard facts of the human side of existence . . . which historians attempt to discover and construct."[11] The second concept is the "perceived past." "This is a much more plastic thing, more capable of being retrospectively reformed by human beings living in the present . . . recorded in memory and writing."[12] He suggests that the first, the past of hard facts, exists, but what that means to the inheritors of a tradition is constantly changing as new facts necessitate reevaluation of our perceptions.[13]

Gerda Lerner offers a modification on Shil's understanding of tradition in her distinction between history and History. When she speaks of history she refers to the unrecorded past; History, on the other hand is the recorded and interpreted past. As she points out, women have always been a part of history.

> History-making, on the other hand, is a historical creation. . . . Until the most recent past, these historians have been men, and what they have recorded is what men have done and experienced and found significant. They have called this History and claimed universality for it.[14]

Women have been kept from History-making, the ordering and interpreting of the past; they have not participated in defining how it is we understand the meaning and purpose of our existence. "Women have been systematically excluded from the enterprise of creating symbol systems . . . they have been excluded from theory-formation."[15] This tension between women's actual historical experience and their exclusion from the process of interpretation she calls the "dialectic of women's history."

Narrative theorists (be they theologians, ethicists, etc.) are in agreement as to the importance of tradition. Meaning-giving is essential to the creation and continuity of civilization, and meaning devolves from tradition. The importance of this for understanding women's narratives cannot be underestimated. As long as women were not part of the tradition in the process of interpretation, the tradition could not be anything other than a distorted view of reality, yet it claimed universality. Until women become part of the process of theory-formation, this claim is invalid.

> Seeing as we have seen, in patriarchal terms, is two dimensional. "Adding women" to the patriarchal framework makes it three-dimensional. But

only when the third dimension is fully integrated and moves with the whole, only when women's vision is equal with men's vision, do we perceive the true relations of the whole and the inner connectedness of the parts.[16]

Before women's vision can be integrated into the patriarchal vision, they must first establish a tradition from which that vision can be extracted. Before we can ask what the meaning of women's lives is, we must know what those lives have been.

The emergence of women as novelists began the process of establishing a tradition for women in two ways. First, their voice became part of the public realm, or part of History as recorded. Secondly, their stories began the process of self-definition, the creation of a tradition, or History as interpretation. In this process, as Nancy Armstrong has demonstrated, they also helped to redefine the existing tradition. In fact, Armstrong's work provides an excellent example of the importance of creating a history for women. If she is correct that the relocation of the ground of truth to the life of the individual can be traced to the development of the domestic woman, then women's lives acquire a political force. However, the result of this movement was the ideology of separate spheres, which maintains the nonpolitical characterization of women's lives and restricts these to the private domain; a paradigm that modern women are still combating. Until the impact of women in the formation of this was written, women's understanding of their past was one of relative powerlessness and insignificance. Armstrong's analysis, however, provides women with a new way of understanding their past that validates claims to moral authority.

Michael Goldberg has claimed that perhaps the most persuasive narratives are biographies and autobiographies. "The importance of narrative is perhaps nowhere more evident and justified than in the portrayal of a life."[17] This is because both claim to be "true to life," that is, the story itself is true, and "this life story holds out some truth about life that the one hearing or reading it can incorporate into or at least relate to his or her own life story."[18] These types of narratives claim to *be* true and to *ring* true. Both provide the examination of a human life as it is acted out within the framework of a paradigmatic narrative and seek to answer the question of what is the meaning of a life within this framework.

With autobiography the issue of truth goes one step further because the reader also must ask about "the truthfulness of the self who writes the story of the self who is."[19] In biography the storyteller is responsible for giving an accurate accounting of the facts. Autobiography reveals more in that we may evaluate the meaning of the story on the basis of the truthfulness of the storyteller. How the autobiographer relates his or her life reveals their understanding of the meaning and intention of their life.

> The standpoint, the determination of what will be recalled and how, gives a life its unity, its coherence, its shape—in short, its story. . . . What is revealed and what remains hidden may say and reveal a good deal about the character of the person writing. . . . It is this very sense of the shaping of the narrative by the writer's perspective on things . . . that awakens the reader's critical judgment of the story, the storyteller, and the credibility of both.[20]

If we consider the history of Western civilization as the male autobiography (since it is the story of men's lives, told by men), women's stories can be understood as a challenge to the credibility of both story and storyteller. They mark the recognition that, as Adrienne Rich has so succinctly put it, the world described by men is not the whole world.[21]

Women's novels challenge the self-deception of the male autobiography. What has been called History is a distortion of the truth. The emergence of women's voice, and the gradual self-definition of that voice, has served to expose the falsehood of the normative claims that History has made. If men really hear this voice it will necessitate the destruction of their basic concept of reality. This is not to say that men and women will share no common perceptions of reality. Modern persons, male and female, are subject to traditions and cannot fully escape them. Although women have not shaped Western tradition, they have surely been subject to its demands. It is impossible to return to an earlier, idyllic age, even if such an age could be authenticated. I am subject, as are all women in our culture, to a part of the tradition that maintains the central significance of the individual, and I have argued that this concept was crucial to the emergence of women's voice. Although I might agree that this may need redefining, I obviously am not willing to reject it. There is, however, one basic concept of masculine reality that women's stories do contradict, and that is the presumed centrality and normative quality of male experience. I will deal with this point in greater depth later in the text.

Such revelation is never easy, and we cannot expect that men will experience this as a blessed epiphany. "The self-deceiver wants us to believe these things about him because he believes them about himself.

. . . Self-deception is . . . *reflexive.*"[22] Self-deception is a means of protecting the integrity of the self when it is confronted with contradiction. The self-deceiver lacks a story which is

> expansive and comprehensive enough to allow them to acknowledge and incorporate disharmonious and unflattering elements into their lives. In short . . . a story that can sustain them in the face of those engagements that seriously challenge the current stories they give themselves."[23]

In commenting on autobiography Dorothy Sayers cautions it is "an infallible self-betrayal."[24] The truth about the writer will make itself known, in spite of any illusions he or she may foster. Should the author attempt to incarnate the self as something other than what it really is, whether or not the deception is deliberate, this will be revealed as falsehood.

As women's stories became increasingly self-definitive, they presented an image that was inconsistent with the male autobiography, and they began to reveal it for the self-deception it was. Women's narratives are not simply an alternative vision that can find congruence with the broader tradition of Western civilization. They were, and continue to be, at the most basic level, a denial of the truth of *the* paradigmatic narrative that has shaped all other narratives we have been heir to.

I will return to this point later, but now I want to consider some of the specific ways that narrative has functioned efficaciously for women and locate these within the broader discussion of narrative theology.

The Mediatory Capacity of Narrative

In chapter three I considered Michael McKeon's argument that the novel was able to serve as a mediator in the social and epistemological crisis of the late seventeenth and eighteenth centuries. Nancy Armstrong argued that the novel was one of the primary means by which the middle-class ideology was constructed, and that it then served to affirm this new ideology. I further suggested that the novel, which had helped to establish the conception of separate spheres, was also the vehicle that was then to enable women to emerge authoritatively into the realm of public moral debate. What is clear is that the novel is able to facilitate transition and change within its structure. It is this capacity of the novel that first makes it effective as a theological construct for women.

The act of creation is, for women, an act of usurpation of traditional groundings of authority. It has been effective because of the public character of the novel and the way in which it is able to take moral and theological claims out of the rarified atmosphere of the academy and into the arena of common debate. Through the use of narrative, women have been able to incorporate and encourage women who might be excluded if such discussions were confined to the domain of pure scholarship. Sayers's novel, for example, dealt with the question of the appropriateness of scholarship as a vocation for women. Although this had been a public debate since the mid-nineteenth century and had been widely argued and reported in the press, by couching it in narrative Sayers was able to approach it from an internal perspective: the heart and mind of Harriet Vane. Readers (both women and men) were made sympathetic to her position and this makes Sayers's argument all the more powerful.

This ability of narrative to mediate not only questions of *how* we ground issues of truth, but also *who* may be a part of this discussion is one of the strengths that has been noted by narrative theologians and theorists. Walter Fisher has compared what he identifies as the "Narrative Paradigm" to the "Rational World Paradigm."[25] The rational world paradigm is characterized by certain presuppositions: the superiority of rational argument (dependent on expertise in a given subject), exposited by means of argumentative skill and informed by a vision of the world as a set of logical puzzles that can be rationally resolved. Fisher continues that the actualization of this paradigm "requires participation of qualified persons. . . ."[26] In other words, being rational, according to the dictates of this model, is something that must be learned. Although this paradigm may function effectively within a closed community—in which everyone is skilled in the necessary requirements and all know the rules by which to participate—it does not function effectively in public moral debate.

Therefore, he offers an alternative to this model: the narrative paradigm. He identifies narrative as "a theory of symbolic actions . . . that have sequence and meaning for those who live, create, or interpret them."[27] Human beings are inherently "symbol-using animals" and stories are created and communicated to order human experience and to establish communities.

The requirements of narrative rationality are such that they provide for greater participation of a given community; it is not necessary to be educated into it; stories are an inherent way of human knowing. As a result, while the rational world paradigm implies a hierarchy, the narrative paradigm is more readily available to the general community and is therefore "inimical to elitist politics," at least theoretically.

The case can be made that as a medium for moral argument, narrative worked particularly well for women because of the different requirement of rationality. Recall Fisher's statement that the rational paradigm requires the participation of qualified persons. The key word is, of course, "qualified." The question must be asked who establishes the criteria for qualification and who certifies qualification? Since the rational world paradigm was defined, refined, and maintained in the male world of academia, the answer is obvious: This was a masculine model. I am not arguing that this kind of rationality is an inherently masculine mode of knowing. Fisher, Goldberg, Hauerwas, and MacIntyre all indicate that it is not; they suggest that this kind of rationality is an artificial model for both men and women. It is, however, a masculine model in that it is a creation of male minds and male-centered institutions.

As women entered the universities they, too, began to be trained in this model. However, the number of university women who were educated according to this paradigm was limited, and they could not assume that there was a wider audience of women who would be capable of, or interested in, this kind of discourse. Additionally, it is about the time that women do begin to make inroads into the masculine preserves that this model begins to falter as a medium for public debate. Since it is elitist in nature, the body of persons who can participate in it is necessarily limited, and as the self-conscious public increased in the nineteenth century, the efficacy of the rational paradigm correspondingly diminished.

Terry Eagleton has argued that the rise in the study of English literature in the Victorian period was due to its capacity to carry forth the middle-class ideology and to inculcate the working class with bourgeois values. He claims, in fact, that literature took the place of religion as the primary means of communicating moral values, and that by the end of the nineteenth century literature had become the "moral ideology for the modern age."[28] Although Eagleton's observations are in the context of an extended discussion of the ideological nature of literature (which I will return to at a later point), his work serves to underscore the ability of the novel to mediate between social groups. Therefore, for the same reasons that Fisher thinks the narrative paradigm is better suited for public moral debate in general, I would maintain that it is also better suited for women's use.

Michael Goldberg suggests that narrative is able to mediate between opposing claims because it addresses the issue of truth in a way that does not demand congruence between all persons. Because narrative is so significant for human lives, Goldberg suggests that the claims we extract from a particular story may be less important than how one justifies a particular reading of the story: How do we know we "got it right?"[29] If we misunderstand the story, any theology that we derive from it will be wrong. Since women's stories present a critique of the patriarchal autobiography, the issue of how one justifies a particular reading of a story is an important one. In a sense women's stories are another interpretation of the Western tradition, but their stories and men's stories differ so radically that it is, in essence, a completely different narrative. The basic difference in men's and women's stories is that men's stories assume the normative quality of men's lives. Therefore they ignore women's experience. One example that comes immediately to mind is the "story" of the Renaissance. As Mary Daly has made clear, this period of European history, which is recalled as an era of enlightenment, is the same period in which thousands, perhaps millions, of women were killed as witches.[30] "Erasure of witches and deletion of the witch-hunters is the name of the game in scholarship 'about women' of the so-called Renaissance and Reformation period in Europe."[31] Which story is true?

Goldberg points out that a failure to hear what the story says will lead to failure to correctly understand the claims that it makes; claims of truth must be made in terms of the story itself. The examination of women's experience through story is not simply the posing of an alternative to the prevailing tradition. It is a challenge to the normative claims of that tradition. The accepted givenness of the past (the patriarchal narrative) leads to the idea that it is natural, and therefore normative.[32] By and large, traditions attain a normative character because they have lasted. As a result, a tradition that has lasted a long time acquires "a certain presumptive evidence of validity."[33]

The claim of women's stories is that the tradition we have inherited is a lie, or at best a partial truth. The truth of women's narratives is the exposure of the lie. Women's narratives are a re-visioning of the tradition and the establishment of a new truth.

In her work on narratives of Black women, Mary Helen Washington makes the following observation about the place of women in our "common" tradition:

Tradition . . . A word that has so often been used to exclude or misrepresent women. . . . What we have to recognize is that the creation of the fiction of tradition is a matter of power, not justice, and that that power has always been in the hands of men. . . . Women are the disinherited.[34]

As Goldberg points out, the truth of a narrative is not dependent on the fact that everyone "gets it." "There will always be some . . . who will miss it for what it is and who will fail to appreciate the kinds of things it has to say."[35] From the time women emerged as writers they have been subject to male critique. Sometimes they were attacked for writing about subjects that were inappropriate to feminine sensibilities (as defined by men). Or they were castigated for writing in a style that was not suited to women (again according to male definition). They have also been, in more recent times, accused of depicting a vision of reality that was distorted or one-sided (of course, men have always done this). This inability of men to understand narratives that derive from women's experience is, of course, rooted in the fact that they don't share that experience. The fact that men were the definers of our literary tradition meant that, for the most part, they could ignore or trivialize women's narratives because they were not congruent with men's experience. "Women's writing is considered singular and anomalous, not universal and representative . . ."[36] This does not mean, however, that the experience is not true. Men are invited to understand women's experience through the telling of women's stories; whether or not they do is not the responsibility of women, nor does their failure to do so negate the truth of the narrative.

Narrative holds the *possibility* of mediation between the world of masculine tradition and women's experience. Because the truth of a narrative does not depend on validation from those who disagree with it, it is possible to enter into debate about opposing claims with the presumption of equality of truth. This, of course, leads to the second aspect of narrative that serves women well: its grounding in the experience of the individual as a foundation for truth.

The Moral Authority of the Individual

The development of the novel was part of a process in which the locus of authority shifted from the tradition of received authority to the life of the autonomous individual. The individual experience of a person came to have increasing significance as a framework for, and means of evaluation of, moral arguments.

The novel's serious concern with the daily lives of ordinary people seems to depend upon two important general conditions: the society must value

every individual highly enough to consider him [sic] the proper subject of
its serious literature; and there must be enough variety of belief and
action among ordinary people for a detailed account of them to be of
interest to other ordinary people, the readers of novels . . . both depend
on the rise of interdependent factors denoted by the term "individualism."[37]

Nancy Armstrong has suggested that the moral authority of the domestic woman was the prototype of the modern individual.

The significance of this epistemological transition for the lives of
women has been discussed. It provided the ground for the emergence
of women's public voice and created a world view in which the claims
of a theologian like Dorothy Sayers—that her experience was a valid
foundation for the development of a theology—were justifiable.

This aspect of story is one that narrative theologians also consider
significant. Michael Goldberg maintains that the truth claims one
extracts from a story must "be appropriate to the *kind of story* which
that theology claims as their ground."[38] Further, the story must be
integral to the meaning; it cannot be discarded once the theological
truth has been extracted. This is a recognition of the interconnectedness of the narrative structure and that the story is revealed through
this. The realization of this truth for women is perhaps best reflected
in the now-familiar phrase, which arose within the women's movement, that "the personal is political." As a challenge to the patriarchal
tradition the emergence of women as novelists is the message. In
writing stories women were not only claiming that there is a truth to
be told, but that the telling of it itself constitutes a truth: Women will
be interpreters and symbol makers. It is, perhaps, for this reason that
Dorothy Sayers chose, as the ultimate attack against the women at
Shrewsbury, the destruction of Miss Lydgate's manuscript: She was
acting as an interpreter and symbol maker.

This is, of course, analogous to Dorothy Sayers's claim that the
experience of the creative artist and the expression of that experience
cannot be separated. The experience can only be fully realized in its
expression.

Goldberg goes on to say that narratives must be interpreted within
the context of the tradition that claims it. If stories are taken out of
their context we "run the risk of seriously misunderstanding them *in
the eyes of the community whose traditional context it is*."[39] Women's
stories claim to describe the experience of women. Novels are, of
course, fictions, and the question can be raised as to whether or not
fiction can claim to be truth. However, although the novel is a fictional
representation, it intends to be a realistic representation.

> . . . [E]verything recounted is required to be credible, or at least to have
> a definite and consistent relation to the facts of existence. . . . No work
> of fiction would be accorded the name of novel unless it were a prose
> story, picturing real life, or something corresponding thereto. . . .[40]

It is a written account that has the basic characteristic of history; a
fictionalized account that is nevertheless accurate to the historical
experience of women. Or, as Michael McKeon puts it, the realism of
the novel "validates literary creation for being not history but history-
like. . . ."[41]

Women's stories are the history-like accounting of women's experience. This is, in part, what made Sayers's story so powerful. Although
it was a work of fiction, it was based on her own historical experience
as a woman scholar. The disclosure of this experience by women
reveals the distortion of the patriarchal narrative and makes a claim
for the truth of the experience. The telling of women's stories is, in
part, the process of creating a tradition for women. But these stories
are grounded in the tradition they are in the process of creating. This
is the tradition of the experience of women's lives, heretofore hidden
in the annals of History, but not nonexistent, which we are now
articulating and claiming.

Claims of this nature constitute both moral and theological argument. Moral argument "is founded on ultimate questions—of life and
death, of how persons should be defined and treated, of preferred
patterns of living."[42] That this is the case with women's novels seems
hardly to need a defense. As women began to examine their lives and
to claim validity for women's experience they challenged prevailing
assumptions about the relative insignificance of this experience. The
very act of writing novels asserted that women had the right to demand
to be heard. This constituted not only debate about how women should
be defined, but was a mandate for self-definition. As women's novels
have increasingly suggested that the male-defined parameters of existence are no longer authoritative, they cannot be construed as anything
other than moral argument.

In addition, as the work of Dorothy Sayers indicates, the creative
work of the author also poses a theological claim. If, as she argues,
human beings image forth the divine nature in acts of creation, then
women's novels suggest that the sacred may be revealed through the
experience of women.

The authority of individual experience that the novel helped to
establish and now presupposes provided a medium through which

women could articulate a contradictory vision of reality, and by which they could validate that vision without reference to the tradition that it opposed. In so doing they were able to communicate an alternative interpretation of humanity that called forth response from other women who shared the same experience. This leads to the final aspect of narrative I wish to consider: its ability to empower others.

The Creative Power of Narrative

Recall Dorothy Sayers's assertion that the power of the creative work and the creative artist is revealed in the capacity to image forth an experience in such a way that others may share in it. The power of the novel to accomplish this is due, in part, to the fact that it is a popular genre. Women who might never pick up a volume of scholarly exposition will read novels. Novels are part of the public domain and are therefore able to communicate across barriers that might otherwise separate individuals.

Narrative, as a particular type of moral argument, does not rely exclusively on the persuasiveness of facts, logic, and so on, but rather generates "good reasons" that are not accounted for in other types of discourse. "These issues include the motivations and values of the characters involved . . . the way in which they conceive and behave in respect to the conflict, and the narrative probability and narrative fidelity of the particular stories. . . ."[43]

The significance of this for understanding women's novels as moral argument is clear. The inclusion of issues such as intentionality enables the reader to assess the examinations of women's lives as more than merely descriptive; it is assumed that they also imply prescriptive analysis. Additionally, since the process negates the dominance of "experts," narrative provides the medium by which women could counter the authority that defined their subordination.

Goldberg has noted that the efficacy of narrative is due to the fact that not only does it claim to be true but it can also "come true" for those who hear it. To be a narrative theology the story must have the power to affect our lives, and therefore it makes claims on us. ". . . [A] narrative that can no longer generate the kind of conviction(s) on which people stake their lives is, in a very real sense, a lifeless story— and ought to be judged accordingly."[44]

The rationality of a narrative arises from the ability to join questions of praxis to the questions of meaning and truth. Or as Fisher puts it, "Narrative rationality . . . offers an account, an understanding, of any instance of human choice and action. . . ."[45] Women's stories reflect the power of the narrative to affect our lives in two ways. Women as *novelists* make claims on other women, and on men, in relationship to men's exclusive claim to creative privilege. Women became creators, and in so doing claimed the right *to be*. They also made claims against the normative patriarchal tradition that reserved this area for men. Elaine Showalter has argued that the power of early women writers rested on the fact that they no longer subscribed to the male-defined identity of the Angel in the House. ". . . [W]omen novelists had authority to describe the lives of ordinary women, those powerless lives of influence, example, and silence, precisely because they had outgrown them. . . ."[46]

Secondly, the revelation of women's experience makes claims on women as *readers* of novels to identify with other women as definers of women's experience. Women novelists, as self-definers, challenged other women to examine the "truth" of patriarchy for themselves: ". . . they were writing not only to develop direct personal power, but also to change the perceptions and aspirations of their female readers."[47] If nothing else, I am sure that Harriet Vane changed the perceptions of at least some readers about academic, independent women.

This is a power that women writers can, and do, still exercise. In my own life this has been made manifestly clear.[48] My self-identification as a feminist is due as much to the influence of women's narratives as it is the result of subsequent scholarship. In fact, I would go so far as to say that the consciousness that made the scholarship possible derived from the impact of significant novels. The effect that Marilyn French's novel *The Women's Room,* a "popular" novel, had on myself and countless other women I know cannot be underestimated.

I would maintain that women's narratives constitute both a moral discourse and a ground for theology. They challenge normative judgments established by the patriarchal tradition as to how human beings should be in the world. They propose an alternative vision of reality, and the very nature of the critique they presuppose is a moral issue. They are a theology for the same reason. The influence of the Judeo-Christian tradition on the development of the history of Western civilization cannot be underestimated. As Gerda Lerner notes, the development of monotheism in Genesis was a major advance of humankind toward abstract thought and universal symbols. However, "the very process of symbol making occurred in a form which marginalized women. For females, the Book of Genesis represented . . . finally the recognition that they were excluded from being able to represent the divine principle."[49] The claim of women to be symbol makers therefore represents a complete overturning of male exclusivity of the sacred. As Dorothy Sayers makes clear, in the act of writing women claim to themselves, also, the divine principle.

NARRATIVE VISION AND THE DUAL VISION OF FEMINISM

The overarching critique voiced by narrative theologians and theorists is a bemoaning of the inheritance of liberal individualism, which has led to a loss of any notion of community or a common good in the modern era. MacIntyre points out that the social world has become "a meeting place for individual wills . . . who understand the world solely as an arena for the achievement of their own satisfaction."[50] We live in a world in which moral arguments have fallen prey to the emotivist critique, and the self presented by emotivism is a "democratised self"; a self who is to be disengaged from any moral position based on particularity. It is a self not rooted in a tradition and whose moral commitments are therefore understood to be arbitrary; a self "distinct on the one hand from its social embodiments and lacking on the other any rational history of its own. . . ."[51] This has led to what another critic has called the "crisis of the political imagination"; characterized by the "dissolution of political communities" and the "attenuation of activity of citizenship."[52] The result is that political theorists have lost their sense of vocation and purpose. Michael Sandel notes that the "rights-based ethics" that are now in ascendency in political theory presuppose a separateness of persons; they are formulated on the assumption of the independent, choosing self.[53] It is this "crisis" that has led Goldberg to ask if the root of our differences is really an unresolvable relativism, and Fisher to suggest the inadequacy of the rational world paradigm for resolving public moral debate. Shils has noted that the modern emphasis on individuality has led to a dread of being encumbered by the past. Rather, the first obligation of the individual, as such, is to find out "who one really is"; to discover the "uncontaminated self."[54]

For narrative theologians, the importance of narrative is in the recovering of a tradition within which we can locate ourselves to create community; it is a communitarian vision, and it is very seductive. Alasdair MacIntyre is perhaps the most able exemplar of this vision, and so it is worthwhile to briefly examine his work, which is rooted in

Aristotelian philosophy. His book, *After Virtue,* is a detailed, closely argued thesis in which he suggests that Aristotle's teleological concept of virtue can be restored. I haven't the time (nor is it necessary) to recount his argument in totality. However, he suggests that there is one virtue that, despite much disagreement regarding the virtues in Western thought, has remained, and that makes no sense without an underlying concept of the wholeness of human life: the virtue of constancy or integrity. According to MacIntyre there was one question that was assumed to have an answer in the premodern world:

> . . . is it rationally justifiable to conceive of each human life as a unity, so that we may try to specify each such life as having its good and so that we may understand the virtues as having their function in enabling an individual to make of his or her life one kind of unity rather than another?[55]

The modern world, he argues, has trouble thinking of life as a unity, and this has both social and philosophical grounds. Socially we have segmented human life and philosophically we tend to think atomistically about human action and to make distinctions between the individual and the roles he or she plays.[56] In light of this fragmentation of the modern mind and life we need to restore a narrative tradition. It is impossible to characterize human behavior independently of intentions, and intentions cannot be characterized independently of their settings. "Narrative history of a certain kind turns out to be the basic and essential genre for the characterisation of human actions."[57]

Without a context human life is unintelligible, and narrative provides this context; this is a common theme in the discussions of narrative theology. As MacIntyre puts it, to ask "What is the good for man [sic]?" is to ask what all the individual answers to "What is the good for me?" have in common. The reason that all modern theories of justice (he cites Rawls and Nozick) appear irresolvable is that they are premised on the modern concept of the individual; there is no place for questions of desert. Notions of desert only work in the context of a community that is bound by a shared understanding of the good for "man" and the good for the community, and where individual interests are identified with reference to these goods.[58]

There are some evident problems with this understanding of community for women; I wish to focus on three—the critique of individualism, the concept of a common good, and the emphasis on meritocracy.

The Critique of Individualism

At the outset this may not appear to be at odds with feminist thought. Feminism has emphasized the problems of failing to see and account for the interconnectedness of human existence. In sources as diverse as *Reweaving the Web of Life*[59] to Toni Morrison's latest novel *Beloved* women have explored the interrelatedness of life and the implications of this for understanding reality.[60]

However, women's emergence as novelists cannot be disassociated from the liberal individualism that the communitarians decry. As one chronicler of narrative has noted:

> The whole movement of mind in Western culture . . . which spawned the novel . . . has been a movement away from dogma, certainty, fixity, and all absolutes in metaphysics, in ethics, and in epistemology. . . . And the novel . . . has played a vital role in the general movement, particularly in calling into question categorical imperatives which society seeks to impose on the ethical behavior of individuals.[61]

The interest in the individual led to the movements here identified and also paved the way for the articulation of women's experience. The dogma and the absolute that characterized an earlier era was the absolute certainty that women "should be seen and not heard." The communal vision of these societies was one that excluded women. The Greek polis of Aristotle, as a community of citizens was, we should recall, a community of men.

The individualism that MacIntyre and others deplore was the vehicle by which women emerged as novelists, and it was through the telling of women's stories that women began to, and are still, defining their voice. As MacIntyre notes, a communitarian ideal necessitates a tradition, and women have not yet completed the task of identifying theirs.

The elevation of the individual cannot, of course, be separated from political liberalism, which was foundational for the middle-class identity of the nineteenth century. We might expect, therefore, that women's narratives would serve the agenda of liberal feminism well.[62] In the nineteenth and early twentieth century this seems to be the case: Women were fighting to be recognized as individual persons. Although Dorothy Sayers did not identify herself as a feminist, she articulated this position when she wrote "What we ask is to be human individuals, however peculiar and unexpected."[63] As a product of the liberal ideology of her age, Sayers was making a plea for the same right to autonomy that men enjoyed. Modern liberal (or moderate) feminism articulates the same basic position. "The main thrust of the liberal feminist's argument is that the individual woman should be able to determine her social role with as great freedom as does a man."[64]

Yet, if I am right about the usurpation of authority that women's novels represented, women's narratives constitute a more radical critique. ". . . [T]he radical feminist does not claim that women should be free to determine their own social roles: she believes instead that the whole 'role system' must be abolished. . . ."[65] Although women's stories may have begun as a claim for an equal place within the system, the authentic inclusion of women is actually a mandate for a complete upheaval of it.

The reason for this is that liberal political theory did not significantly alter preconceived notions about women's social role. It would have been difficult, in fact, for liberalism to have done so, given its compatibility with middle-class ideology, which in the nineteenth century served to establish the concept of separate spheres.

Liberal thought assumes that the least possible government intervention into private lives is the most desirable state of affairs. Due to the separation of spheres, sexual relations were defined as part of the private realm and were therefore "untouchable" by political institutions.[66] "In doing so, liberals have left uncriticized laws that enforce with respect to gender the institutionalization of the notion of a natural place assigned by birth which, when applied to class, was the original target of liberal theory."[67]

However, the emergence of women as novelists—as symbol makers and interpreters—while appearing to be simply an inclusion of women in the liberal agenda, actually goes far beyond this. It established gender as a political category and can therefore be recognized as a claim for political and social power.

Terry Eagleton has argued that what constitutes "literature" is dependent on value judgments: "Literature" turns out to be "a highly valued kind of writing."[68] Therefore it is not objective nor, since value judgments change, is it constant. "Literature . . . *is* an ideology. It has the most intimate relations to questions of social power."[69]

The rising moral authority of literature in the nineteenth century, he argues, was due to a corresponding decline in the authority of religion as the communicator of moral values. Literature eventually usurped religion. Religion had been the exclusive preserve of men, and so, therefore, had moral authority. However, as women began to write, they entered into the new arena of moral debate. The early disdain with which the universities viewed English literature made it more easily accessible to women; ". . . it seemed a convenient sort of non-subject to palm off on the ladies. . . ."[70] Nevertheless, English literature eventually was established as a serious discipline. "In the early 1920s it was desperately unclear why English was worth studying at all; by the early 1930s it had become a question of why it was worth wasting your time on anything else."[71]

As literature gained academic credibility, men sought to regain control over its authority, and the canon of literature that was established was predominantly masculine. However, women had begun to write, and although their narratives were not recognized by men (with very few exceptions), they were not silenced and their voice gained in power and authority. Modern feminist scholarship has called attention to the exclusion of women from the canon, and women are being written back into the tradition of literature. As this occurs, and as women continue to write, the authority of the patriarchal narrative continues to be called into question.

For this reason I would maintain that although the emergence of women as individuals may appear, on the surface, to be a bid for a place within the existing social system, at a more fundamental level it is a denial of the reality that that system represents.

The Ideal of the Common Good

As MacIntyre makes clear, the concept of a common good necessitates being able to define our individual goods, and then finding congruence between them. We cannot know what we have in common until we know wherein lie our differences. To ask "What is the good for humanity?" we must ask "What is the good for women?" and "What is the good for men?", although, of course, the good for men has been made abundantly clear throughout our history. But only after women have been able to clearly articulate their "good" can we begin to ask such questions as "Which are we willing to forego to establish communal goals?"

In order to enter this debate a tradition is necessary; a history of identifying goods and of making choices between options. This is a tradition men have but that women have shared in only as receivers, not as shapers. Therefore, we cannot assume that it represents a common good. As I have said, women are still creating, or discovering their history. Until we can say with certainty "This is our tradition" and know that what we point to is not simply a response to oppression (which is still the definition of women in terms of men's lives), but is also the enactment of women's legitimate choice and expression, we must beware of the common good. We run the danger of being, once again, subsumed under a masculine category that we have not defined.

There is a natural tendency to welcome inclusion in the male community. Women have, for so long, existed only on the periphery, as outsiders looking in, that the invitation to join the group appears to be a battle won. However, as Gerda Lerner explains in a theatrical analogy, "It takes considerable time for the women to understand that getting 'equal' parts will not make them equal, as long as the script, the props, the stage setting, and the direction are firmly held by men."[72] The communitarian vision is still a vision defined by a tradition of patriarchy. Women have perhaps been invited to share it, but they have not been asked to define it. Because of their position as outsiders, women's understanding of the tradition, grounded in an experience of it that men do not share, is viewed with suspicion. "In all the works of interpretation there are insiders and outsiders, the former . . . professing to have immediate access to the mystery, the latter . . . excluded from the elect who mistrust or despise their unauthorized divinations. . . ."[73]

According to Goldberg, although there is a place for propositional theology, it is limited by the experience of life, "for as its propositions are abstracted and drawn from life, so too, in the end, they must return to life and have meaning for life in order to be theologically significant."[74] As theologians, men have had a common life history from which to extract and to which they could return in such a way that their theologies made sense. Women were expected to, and for the most part did, share in these theologies. They were part of men's communities but did not participate in them in the same way men did. The experience of women under patriarchy was a very different experience than that of men. Therefore, although women shared in the propositional theologies of men, abstracted from men's lives, they could not return these to their own life experiences and have the same awareness of congruence. Judith Plaskow has examined such an instance in her assessment that the definition of the "sin of man" as pride is not consistent with women's experience of self-negation.[75]

Women need new propositional theologies but they must first define their own tradition. This is, in part, a redefinition of the patriarchal tradition from the viewpoint of outsiders and will therefore appear to the insiders as misinterpretation. But this is more than just a reinterpretation of the existing tradition; it is also the creation of a new one.

I understand this as being akin to Carol Christ's assertion that women begin from the experience of nothingness.[76] As Christ has made clear, women are reminded of the nothingness of their existence in countless ways within patriarchy. Men, on the other hand, begin with and return to the experience of being. Women must create a tradition in which they *are*, and to which they can return. This is not simply a reinterpretation of what it means to be a woman as defined by patriarchy. It is the creation of a tradition defined by the experience of

> those women who have been for women, those who have lived for women's freedom and those who have died for it; those who have fought for women and survived by women's strength; those who have loved women and who have realized that without the consciousness and conviction that women are primary in each other's lives, nothing else is in perspective.[77]

This vision will be considered suspect because it is one in which men are not central, and the presumed centrality and normative quality of masculine existence is the foundation of patriarchy.

This suspicion is reflected in Goldberg's question "Are we left with the grim possibility of a Carol Christ telling men that they cannot hope to appreciate or evaluate theologies based on women's stories?"[78] I have some ideas as to why Goldberg thinks this is a "grim possibility" to which I will return shortly.

This suspicion is also reflected in critiques often leveled at women's narratives. Mary Washington observed that women's writing is thought to be "singular and anomalous" rather than "universal and representative." The reason for this is obvious. Because men did not share women's experience, they therefore assumed it was not universal, and was therefore of less value than the experience articulated by men.

Masculine criticism has maintained that great literature (and art, and music) is great precisely because it does represent universal themes, and taken at face falue this seems a logical assessment. The reason we value certain literature is because of its ability to speak across barriers of time, place, and social location. What has not been taken into account is whose universe was functioning as the paradigm. Men assumed their universe was normative and remained oblivious to the universe next door, which was inhabited by women. As women began to articulate the reality of their lives through narrative, this hidden universe was brought into public view.

Narrative theologians are now faced with the problems deriving from the individualism that is part of the modern world, and are asking what "social glue" can possibly hold a society together when each person in that society is governed by a principle of radical individuality? Wherein lies our commonality? What is universal? However, until women's experience is no longer considered singular and anamolous, women's concern is not commonality but differentiation. What are women's lives like? What do we, as women, share? The task is first to establish the legitimacy of our universe. Mary Washington has argued that "The making of a literary history in which black women are fully represented is a search for full vision, to create a circle where now we have but a segment."[79] Black women labor, of course, under the double burden of racism and sexism. While I in no way intend to minimize their oppression, I believe Washington's insight can be applied to all women in general.

Women's narratives began the search for a full vision for women. The task will not be complete, however, until women's experience is thought of as human experience, even though it is different from the "universal" experience of men.

The fact that this difference in experience exists leads to one final danger with the concept of a common good. I accept Carol Christ's argument that women begin from a position of nothingness in patriarchal society. This implies that men's and women's narratives reflect a different concept of the good. For men, the search for community must begin with a denial of the ego-centered self, as evidenced by the narrative critique of individualism. Community represents the ability of one man to transcend his self to embrace the good of others.

Women's narratives are, on the other hand, a quest to find the self to which patriarchy has denied existence. Women know what it is to sacrifice their lives for others; what is difficult is accepting oneself as a legitimate claimant when there is a conflict of interests. Membership in a community, for women, must begin with recognition of the self, and women's stories are about discovering and validating this self.

The danger of the communitarian vision is that it proceeds from an assumption that all individuals are overly concerned with self-interest and therefore require a narrative paradigm that will mitigate against this tendency. Women are still discovering that self-interest is legitimate. The narrative paradigm that serves women well, then, is one that celebrates women's autonomy.

Meritocracy

According to MacIntyre, the concept of desert in a discussion of justice is tied to a recognition of a common good. To ask what one deserves from a society is to ask what one has given to that society: reward according to merit. In Aristotle's teleological philosophy all natural things have ends that are inherent in the whole, and this extends to human beings. This is why he could speak of persons deserving reward according to merit. He assumes that personal merit is something that is the natural end of a person's makeup. However, his empirical approach to questions of truth did not allow for categories we now speak of when asking questions of social justice; categories such as economic inequalities, social disadvantage, and so on. The ability of the individual to contribute to society is related to the "goods" one has, and this is often beyond our control.

Even more significant is the issue of how these "goods" are defined and by whom. What is good for society, under patriarchy, has not been good for women. It might be helpful to distinguish between social goods and the social good. There are many goods men have articulated that women share; this is a point I will return to shortly. However, *the* good of patriarchy, the foundation on which it rests, is the presumption that men, by nature, deserve to rule, order, and define society, including women. For women's contributions to be valued they must conform to the tradition, and this is the root of the problem. The "good" for women is inimical to the "good" of society as it now exists. The good for women is the power of self-definition.

I should note at this point that narrative theologians would probably respond to these issues by claiming that they are not unresolvable. They all maintain that part of the tradition is that the tradition is always changing. As MacIntyre puts it, "A living tradition . . . is a historically extended, socially embodied argument, and an argument precisely in part about the goods which constitute that tradition."[80] Goldberg maintains that it is possible to have rational disagreement between our stories,[81] and Fisher believes that narratives are able to bridge the gap between rival factions.[82] Hauerwas reiterates this when he says that "Moral growth involves a constant conversation between our stories. . . ."[83] Tradition appears to all as something that is flexible, that in its very nature is always subject to amendment. "There is something in tradition which calls forth a desire to change it by making improvements in it. . . . However great and indispensible . . . it will not be adequate to answer all the questions of its heirs."[84]

Of course, it can be pointed out that the necessity they all seem to feel to allow for rival stories is the inheritance of the liberalism they deplore and serves to remind us that it is virtually impossible to escape entirely from one's tradition. "Those who hate contemporary society and who declare that they wish to abolish it are often attached to the traditional society which they say they abhor and their rebellion is often limited in range. . . ."[85]

However, perhaps the reason they assume that reconciliation, or at least "rational disagreement" is possible is that they all share an even longer, more overarching tradition—patriarchy. And this is the heart of the problem for women with the communitarian vision. The feminist critique of patriarchy challenges the very basis of the Western concept of reality—the normative character of masculine experience. The fact that this vision grounds itself in Aristotelian philosophy is especially telling.

As Lerner notes, classical Greek society was thoroughly patriarchal and the fact of women's legal and social subordination is undisputed.[86] Citizenship, which was originally based on military participation, was defined so as to exclude women. Masculine superiority was reflected in misogynist characterizations of women and in the doctrine of male procreativity, which was most fully developed by Aristotle. It is his formulation that has had the most lasting effect on Western science and philosophy. His philosophical thought cannot be separated from his biological work, in which women are described as "mutilated men," and where woman's biological inferiority is foundational to her inability to reason. "Aristotle's world view is both hierarchical and dichotomized."[87] As reason rules emotion and appetite, so do masters rule slaves, men rule women, and so on; by "nature" each subordinate group occupies its particular place in the hierarchy. Human society is divided into two sexes: men who are fit to rule, and women who are to be ruled. Men who rule other men (slaves) do so because of the ways in which slaves are like women. Aristotle legitimates class dominance as a logical extension of his gender definitions.

> The fact that sex dominance antedates class dominance and lies at its foundation is . . . most explicit . . . in the way his gender definitions and prescriptions are built into his discourse on politics. . . . The partiarchal family is the cell out of which the larger body of patriarchal dominance arises. Sexual dominance underlies class and race dominance.[88]

The subordination of women is a cornerstone of Aristotelian philosophy and serves as the basis for his understanding of political life. The polis of Aristotle is dependent on the oppression of women. That MacIntyre and others do not acknowledge this aspect of Aristotelian political thought is indicative of the pervasiveness of patriarchy. I have no doubt that MacIntyre would maintain that of course Aristotle's misogyny should not be part of the character of community. The question is, can the two be separated? Lerner indicates that they cannot. Even if it were theoretically possible, the fact remains that the foundational conception of community as articulated by Aristotle is an expressed hatred of women, and for this reason alone must be rejected. This model of communitarian unity is a model that women cannot claim. The vision of community that narrative theorists articulate, whether theologically or philosophically based, is one founded on a tradition that excluded women by definition. "The theologians and the religious institutions say how necessary it is . . . to remain faithful to that with which they have been entrusted. . . . But nostalgically the patriarchal religions evoke the old community in which woman was and is invisible."[89]

The feminist critique is not a modification of the patriarchal narrative tradition that underscores the communitarian ideal. It is a complete upheaval of it. "What women must do . . . [is] say . . . the basic inequality between us lies within this framework. And then they must tear it down."[90]

Male narrative theology is concerned with rebuilding the very sense of community that feminist theorists are in the process of tearing down. Perhaps this is why Michael Goldberg finds it grim. The masculine concept of unity is a concept of oneness, a wholeness of vision. Although there may be differences, there can be unity in spite of these. What this implies is that the differences between rival factions are not so great that they cannot be resolved, or at least that rational disagreement can be achieved. The reason for this is that they all share an unquestioned grounding in patriarchy, which provides all men with a common cause.

> A community is a group of persons who share a history and whose common set of interpretations about the history provide the basis for common actions. These interpretations may be quite diverse and controversial even within the community, but are sufficient to provide the individual members with the sense that they are more alike than unalike.[91]

Dorothy Sayers argued that the reason men do not perceive women as human is that to the careless observer they appear to be different. However, she maintains that women are more like men than anything else because they are both human. At the level of the question of being I am prepared to agree with Sayers, but in terms of the experience of women and men in the tradition of Western culture, it is arguable that we are more unlike than alike. Therefore, although men can find common ground to resolve differences, I am not sure this is the case for men *and* women together.

There are, of course, many goods that men and women hold together in our society. Men and women share an ecological concern that we are exhausting the natural resources of the planet. There are also men who espouse the concern of many women about the destructive character of militarism. Men also have pointed to the rampant consumerism and the exploitation of women through pornography as serious social concerns, and feminists share this perspective. However, patriarchy as *the* good becomes a starting point for feminist analysis because until it is finally overturned, women's voice and experience will never be powerful enough to enter into these debates in a way that can effectively change reality. In fact, as some feminists have argued, the case can be made that these social ills are the result of a culture that has largely been determined by a male perspective. The ideal of patriarchy, which excluded women's perspective, has resulted in a distorted and destructive vision of reality.

CONCLUSION

What I am suggesting is that, in fact, there may be no "common good." To one schooled in the tradition of Western thought this appears intolerable. Elisabeth Young-Bruehl has suggested the feminist critique is a questioning of the very foundations of knowledge—how, and by whom, it has been formed.[92] Both Greco-Roman philosophy and Judeo-Christian theology are grounded in a concept of a single ordering force or mind. This has resulted in the mind/body dualism that is reflected in the male/female distinction. As she states, it is simply not enough to reformulate this dualism in a way that favors women (such as the assertion that women's bodily existence gives her a superior relationship to reality).

> Both restoration of women's voices suppressed in the history of the cultural discourses and restoration of the pluralities of voices inside us that have been threatened with monism in our upbringings and in our encounters with the cultural discourses require analyses of those thought forms and habits of construction. . . .[93]

Until women have clearly identified and understood reality from a distinctly women's perspective, we cannot begin to think about commonality. The feminist critique suggests that there can be no common good as it has been understood within the patriarchal tradition. It cuts to the heart of the most foundational constructs of human thought. As Janice Raymond notes "The history of philosophy is the history of men's reflection about the scheme of things and the relations between things."[94] The world in which we live is characterized by "hetero-reality" in which "women's work, like woman herself, is perceived as derivative."[95]

The vision of community is seductive. Women have been so long excluded that the invitation to "belong" seems enticing. Additionally, feminist work has focused on the fostering of community among women. Raymond's work is precisely this; an examination of how women can build a sense of self and can learn to love each other.

The word community is a powerful one. It seems to call us to that which is the best in us; to challenge us to transcend those things that separate us and cause us to live in a world at odds. However, as Nelle Morton reminds us, "Words do more than signify. They conjure images. . . . Images, therefore, are infinitely more powerful than concepts. Concepts can be learned . . . corrected . . . made precise . . . formulated, enclosed, and controlled. . . . Images, on the other hand, cannot be so controlled."[96]

We need to ask what is being conjured by the masculine image of community. It is a vision of cooperation toward a common good, but have they *heard* that patriarchy is not the common good? Until they do hear this, there is no such thing. We may have to live with Goldberg's "grim possibility" for yet a while longer. "What women are after has been for so many centuries programmed out of these men's lives that their hearing is diminished. . . . I am arguing, at this point in history, for separateness. But . . . separateness is a tactic, and not the end goal."[97]

The concept of community is grounded in a tradition, the memories of which are very different for men and women. For men it has been a tradition of empowerment; for women it has been at best a circum-scribed participation and at worst oppression. It is no wonder that for men it appears as a "golden age." However, Edward Shils cautions us about such perceptions.

> The belief that mankind had once lived in a "golden age," simpler and purer than the one in which it now lives is a common theme in intellectual history. . . . It might be an attachment to the ideal of a whole social order and culture . . . [or] to a particular idea . . . or to a particular pattern of

relationships. The remoteness from a repugnant present is often one of the features of this attraction. . . . The past is a haven to the spirit which is not at ease in the present.[98]

He further goes on to note that proposals to return to such a golden age are usually the project of intellectuals and most often have little effect.[99] The reason for this is that once a tradition has fallen from regular use it cannot be restored. "What will appear will be a fanatical distortion of the received tradition . . . which cannot last . . . because those to whom it is offered or on whom it is imposed will not find it congenial to their circumstances and tastes."[100]

The vision of the common good that is currently being offered is not one that is congenial to women. Whether or not there can someday be a version of the common good that is amenable to both men and women has yet to be determined. In the meantime, women's novels—the stories of women's experience—are powerful tools for creating a memory and a tradition that is distinctly women's. They do this in two ways. First they remind us of our common experience and help to create bridges between women who have been divided by the hetero-reality of our world. Second, they build a body of literature, a well of memories, which become part of the tradition, or as Lerner calls it, History.

As Raymond reminds us, women are still living in the man-made world, but we exist in this world as an "inside outsider." This is "the dual tension of women who see the man-made world for what it is and exist in it with worldly integrity, while at the same time seeing beyond it to something different."[101] This dual vision of feminism suggests a method for appropriating women's novels as theological expression. As women living inside men's world we must ask whether the stories we tell are an accurate depiction of that world. Narratives that romanticize it, minimize the pervasiveness of patriarchy, or ignore its destructive character are not "true" stories. We must be true to, and give a truthful account of, that world. Much "popular feminism" denies the hetero-reality of our world. In recent years there has been a rash of novels in which women are given better parts, but in which the script, set, props, and plot are still defined by male experience. These stories depict the "liberated woman" as a woman who encounters and overcomes the challenges of life as men would; women who live according to the patriarchal definition. These characters play the game and win, but always playing by men's rules. The meaning derived from such stories is that reality defined by masculine experience is still normative. These novels cannot be thought of as the basis for a feminist theology.

As outsiders our narratives need to form the basis of a refusal to be defined by patriarchy. In so doing we can send a message to those men who choose to hear that the world is no longer exclusively theirs. Of even greater significance, women continue the process of self-definition; of creating and establishing women's tradition.

> When women avert their eyes from men, men will have to see each other for what they really are. This may be the beginning of men's salvation or final self-destruction. More important, when women turn their eyes toward their Selves and other women, they put the world in perspective. . . . Women can choose their line of vision. Women can choose to see each other.[102]

The efficacy of the novel that truthfully tells women's story is that it enables us to see other women. As such it empowers and strengthens us, and creates a community between us. It does not create common cause with patriarchal society. It should not be understood as the foundation for the "common good."

NOTES

1. Edward Shils, *Tradition* (Chicago: The University of Chicago Press, 1981), 50.
2. Gerda Lerner, *The Creation of Patriarchy* (New York: Oxford University Press, 1986), 218.
3. Stanley Hauerwas, *A Community of Character* (Notre Dame, Ind.: University of Notre Dame Press, 1981), 9.
4. Walter R. Fisher, "Narration as a Human Communication Paradigm: The Case of Public Moral Argument," *Communication Monographs* 51 (March 1984): 3.
5. Shills, *Tradition,* 43.
6. Alasdair MacIntyre, *After Virtue* (Notre Dame, Ind.: University of Notre Dame Press, 1981), 201.
7. Michael Goldberg, *Theology and Narrative: A Critical Introduction* (Nashville: Abingdon, 1981, 1982), 95.
8. Shils, *Tradition,* 166.
9. Goldberg, *Theology and Narrative,* 145.
10. When using the term patriarchy I employ Lerner's broad definition of

the word: ". . . the manifestation and institutionalization of male dominance over women and children in the family and the extension of male dominance over women in society in general. It implies that men hold power in all the important institutions of society and that women are deprived of access to such power." Lerner, *Creation of Patriarchy*, 239.

11. Shils, *Tradition*, 195.

12. Shils, *Tradition*, 195.

13. Shils, *Tradition*, 196–99.

14. Lerner, *Creation of Patriarchy*, 4.

15. Lerner, *Creation of Patriarchy*, 4.

16. Lerner, *Creation of Patriarchy*, 12.

17. Goldberg, *Theology and Narrative*, 62.

18. Goldberg, *Theology and Narrative*, 63–64.

19. Goldberg, *Theology and Narrative*, 96.

20. Goldberg, *Theology and Narrative*, 98–99.

21. Adrienne Rich, *On Lies, Secrets, and Silence* (New York: W. W. Norton & Company, 1979), 207.

22. Goldberg, *Theology and Narrative*, 107.

23. Goldberg, *Theology and Narrative*, 106.

24. Dorothy L. Sayers, *The Mind of the Maker* (New York: Harcourt, Brace and Company, 1941), 91.

25. Fisher, "Narration," 1–21.

26. Fisher, "Narration," 4.

27. Fisher, "Narration," 2.

28. Terry Eagleton, *Literary Theory: An Introduction* (Minneapolis: University of Minnesota Press, 1983), 27.

29. Goldberg, *Theology and Narrative*, 189.

30. Mary Daly, "European Witchburnings: Purifying the Body of Christ," in Mary Daly, *Gyn/Ecology: The Metaethics of Radical Feminism* (Boston: Beacon Press, 1978), 178–222.

31. Daly, "European Witchburnings," 209.

32. Shils, *Tradition*, 200.

33. Shils, *Tradition*, 204.

34. Mary Helen Washington, ed., *Invented Lives: Narratives of Black Women 1860–1960* (Garden City, N.Y.: Anchor Press, Doubleday & Company, Inc., 1987), xvii–xviii.

35. Goldberg, *Theology and Narrative*, 226.

36. Washington, ed., *Invented Lives*, xix.

37. Ian Watt, *The Rise of the Novel* (Berkeley: University of California Press, English Edition; London: Chatto and Windus Ltd., 1957), 60.

38. Goldberg, *Theology and Narrative*, 201.

39. Goldberg, *Theology and Narrative*, 207.

40. Ernest A. Baker, *The History of the English Novel*, vol. 1, *The Age of Romance: From the Beginnings to the Renaissance* (New York: Barnes & Noble, Inc., 1957), 11.

41. Michael McKeon, *The Origins of the English Novel 1600–1740* (Baltimore: The Johns Hopkins University Press, 1987), 120.

42. Fisher, "Narration," 12.

43. Fisher, "Narration," 13.

44. Goldberg, *Theology and Narrative,* 229–30.

45. Fisher, "Narration," 9.

46. Elaine Showalter, *A Literature of Their Own* (Princeton, N.J.: Princeton University Press, 1977), 99.

47. Showalter, *Literature,* 99.

48. Although personal experience does not, as a rule, satisfy the demands of proof in a scholarly work, since I am making a case for the experiential ground of women's narrative theology, I take this liberty.

49. Lerner, *Creation of Patriarchy,* 198.

50. MacIntyre, *After Virtue,* 24.

51. MacIntyre, *After Virtue,* 31.

52. Bruce Jennings, "Tradition and the Politics of Remembering," *The Georgia Review* 36, no. 1 (Spring 1982): 167–8.

53. Michael J. Sandel, "Morality and the Liberal Ideal," *The New Republic* (7 May 1984): 15–17.

54. Shils, *Tradition,* 10–11.

55. MacIntyre, *After Virtue,* 189.

56. MacIntyre, *After Virtue,* 190.

57. MacIntyre, *After Virtue,* 194.

58. MacIntyre, *After Virtue,* 227–37.

59. See Pam McAllister, ed., *Reweaving the Web of Life: Feminism and Nonviolence* (Philadelphia: New Society Publishers, 1982).

60. See Toni Morrison, *Beloved* (New York: Alfred A. Knopf, 1987).

61. Robert Scholes and Robert Kellogg, *The Nature of Narrative* (New York: Oxford University Press, 1966), 276.

62. The position of liberal, as well as other types of feminist philosophy, is outlined in Alison Jaggar, "Political Philosophies of Women's Liberation," *Feminism and Philosophy*, ed. Mary Vetterling-Braggin, Frederick A. Elliston, and Jane English (Totowa, N.J.: Rowman and Littlefield, 1977), 5–21.

63. Dorothy L. Sayers, "Are Women Human?," in Dorothy L. Sayers, *Are Women Human?* (Grand Rapids, Mich.: William B. Eerdmans Publishing Company, 1971), 29.

64. Jaggar, "Political Philosophies," in *Feminism and Philosophy,* ed. Vetterling-Braggin, Elliston, and English, 6–7.

65. Jaggar, "Political Philosophies," 13.

66. Sara Ann Ketchum, "Liberalism and Marriage Law," in *Feminism and Philosophy,* ed. Mary Vetterling-Braggin, Frederick A. Ellison, and Jane English (Totowa, N.J.: Rowman and Littlefield, 1977), 264–76.

67. Ketchum, "Marriage Law," 264.

68. Eagleton, *Literary Theory,* 10.

69. Eagleton, *Literary Theory*, 22.

70. Eagleton, *Literary Theory*, 28. I discussed this tendency in greater depth in chapter three.

71. Eagleton, *Literary Theory*, 31.

72. Lerner, *Creation of Patriarchy*, 13.

73. Frank Kermode, *The Genesis of Secrecy: On the Interpretation of Narrative* (Cambridge, Mass.: Harvard University Press, 1979), xi.

74. Goldberg, *Theology and Narrative*, 95.

75. See Judith Plaskow, *Sex, Sin and Grace: Women's Experience and the Theologies of Reinhold Niebuhr and Paul Tillich* (Lanham, Md.: University Press of America, 1980).

76. Carol Christ, "Nothingness, Awakening, Insight, New Naming," in Carol Christ, *Diving Deep and Surfacing: Women Writers on Spiritual Quest* (Boston: Beacon Press, 1980), 13–26.

77. Janice G. Raymond, *A Passion for Friends: Toward a Philosophy of Female Affection* (Boston: Beacon Press, 1986), 13.

78. Goldberg, *Theology and Narrative*, 19–20.

79. Washington, *Invented Lives*, xxvii.

80. MacIntyre, *After Virtue*, 107.

81. Goldberg, *Theology and Narrative*, 239.

82. Fisher, "Narration," 14.

83. Hauerwas, *Community of Character*, 133.

84. Shils, *Tradition*, 214.

85. Shils, *Tradition*, 40.

86. Lerner discusses life in classical Greece and the impact of Aristotelian philosophy on women in chapter ten, *Creation of Patriarchy*, 202–11.

87. Lerner, *Creation of Patriarchy*, 208.

88. Lerner, *Creation of Patriarchy*, 209.

89. Nelle Morton, *The Journey is Home* (Boston: Beacon Press, 1985), xxiii.

90. Lerner, *Creation of Patriarchy*, 13.

91. Hauerwas, *Community of Character*, 60.

92. Elisabeth Young-Bruehl, "The Education of Women as Philosophers," *Signs* 12, no. 2 (Winter 1987): 207–21.

93. Young-Bruehl, "Women as Philosophers," 220–21.

94. Raymond, *Passion for Friends*, 19.

95. Raymond, *Passion for Friends*, 4.

96. Morton, *Journey is Home*, 20.

97. Morton, *Journey is Home*, xxvi.

98. Shils, *Tradition*, 206–7.

99. Shils, *Tradition*, 210.

100. Shils, *Tradition*, 329.

101. Raymond, *Passion for Friends*, 232.

102. Raymond, *Passion for Friends*, 241.

Bibliography

Abrams, M. H., E. Talbot Donaldson, Hallett Smith, Robert M. Adams, Samuel Holt Monk, Lawrence Lipking, George H. Ford, and David Daiches, eds. *The Norton Anthology of English Literature.* 3d ed. New York: W. W. Norton & Company, Inc., 1974.

Anderson, Margaret L. *Thinking About Women: Sociological and Feminist Perspectives.* New York: Macmillan Publishing Co., 1983.

Armstrong, Nancy. *Desire and Domestic Fiction: A Political History of the Novel.* New York: Oxford University Press, 1987.

Auerbach, Nina. *Woman and the Demon: The Life of a Victorian Myth.* Cambridge, Mass.: Harvard University Press, 1982.

Baker, Ernest A. *The History of the English Novel.* Vol. 1, *The Age of Romance: From the Beginnings to the Renaissance.* New York: Barnes & Noble, Inc., 1957.

Bell, Susan Groag, and Karen M. Offen, eds. *Women, the Family, and Freedom: The Debate in Documents.* Vol. 1, 1750–1880. Stanford, Calif.: Stanford University Press, 1983.

Brabazon, James. *Dorothy L. Sayers.* New York: Charles Scribner's Sons, 1981.

Branca, Patricia. *Silent Sisterhood: Middle-Class Women in the Victorian Home.* Pittsburgh: Carnegie-Mellon University Press, 1975.

Brittain, Vera. *The Women at Oxford: A Fragment of History.* London: George G. Harrap & Co. Ltd., 1960.

Chadwick, Owen. *The Victorian Church.* Part 2. London: Adam & Charles Black, Ltd., 1970.

Christ, Carol P. *Diving Deep and Surfacing: Women Writers on Spiritual Quest.* Boston: Beacon Press, 1980.

143

Cominos, Peter T. "Innocent Femina Sensualis in Unconscious Conflict." In *Suffer and Be Still: Women in the Victorian Age*, edited by Martha Vicinus, 155–72. Bloomington: Indiana University Press, 1972.

Dale, Alzina Stone. *The Story of Dorothy L. Sayers*. Grand Rapids, Mich.: William B. Eerdmans Publishing Company, 1978.

Daly, Mary. *Gyn/Ecology: The Metaethics of Radical Feminism*. Boston: Beacon Press, 1978.

Daly, Mary, in cahoots with Jane Caputi. *Websters' First New Intergallactic Wickedary of the English Language*. Boston: Beacon Press, 1987.

Dunbar, Janet. *The Early Victorian Woman: Some Aspects of Her Life (1837–57)*. London: George G. Harrap & Co., Ltd., 1953.

Dunn, Robert Paul. " 'The Laughter of the Universe': Dorothy L. Sayers and the Whimsical Vision." In *As Her Whimsey Took Her: Critical Essays on the Work of Dorothy L. Sayers*, edited by Margaret P. Hannay, 200–12. Kent, Ohio: The Kent State University Press, 1979.

Eagleton, Terry. *Literary Theory: An Introduction*. Minneapolis: University of Minnesota Press, 1983.

Engle, A. J. *From Clergyman to Don*. Oxford: Clarendon Press, 1983.

Ewbank, Inga-Stina. *Their Proper Sphere: A Study of the Brontë Sisters as Early-Victorian Female Novelists*. Cambridge, Mass.: Harvard University Press, 1966.

Fisher, Walter R. "Narration as a Human Communication Paradigm: The Case of Public Moral Argument." *Communication Monographs* 51 (March 1984): 1–21.

Gaillard, Dawson. *Dorothy L. Sayers*. New York: Frederick Ungar Publishing Co., 1981.

Gallagher, Catherine. *The Industrial Reformation of English Fiction: Social Discourse and Narrative Form 1832–1867*. Chicago: The University of Chicago Press, 1985.

Gay, Peter. *The Bourgeois Experience: Victoria to Freud*. Vol. 1, *Education of the Senses*. New York and Oxford: Oxford University Press, 1984.

Goldberg, Michael. *Theology and Narrative: A Critical Introduction*. Nashville: Abington, 1981.

Gorham, Deborah. *The Victorian Girl and the Feminine Ideal*. Bloomington: Indiana University Press, 1982.

Graff, Gerald. *Literature Against Itself*. Chicago: The University of Chicago Press, 1979.

Green, V. H. H. *Religion at Oxford and Cambridge*. London: SCM Press, Ltd., 1964.

Hannay, Margaret P., ed. *As Her Whimsey Took Her: Critical Essays on the*

Work of Dorothy L. Sayers. Kent, Ohio: The Kent State University Press, 1979.

Harp, Richard L. "*The Mind of the Maker*: The Theological Aesthetic of Dorothy Sayers and Its Application to Poetry." In *As Her Whimsey Took Her: Critical Essays on the Work of Dorothy L. Sayers*, edited by Margaret P. Hannay, 176–99. Kent, Ohio: The Kent State University Press, 1979.

Harth, Erica. Review of *The Bourgeois Experience*, by Peter Gay. *Science and Society* 48 (Fall 1984): 376–79.

Hauerwas, Stanley. *A Community of Character*. Notre Dame, Ind.: University of Notre Dame Press, 1981.

Heeney, Brian. "The Beginnings of Church Feminism: Women and the Councils of the Church of England, 1879–1919." In *Religion in the Lives of English Women*, edited by Gail Malmgreen, 260–84. Bloomington: Indiana University Press, 1986.

Heilbrun, Carolyn. "Sayers, Lord Peter and God." In *Lord Peter: A Collection of All the Lord Peter Wimsey Stories*, edited by James Sandoe, 454–69. New York: Harper & Row Publishers, 1972.

Hitchman, Janet. *Such a Strange Lady*. New York: Harper & Row Publishers, 1975.

Hobson, J. A. *John Ruskin: Social Reformer*. Boston: Dana Estes & Company, 1898.

Hollis, Patricia. *Women in Public 1850–1900: Documents of the Victorian Women's Movement*. London: George Allen & Unwin, 1979.

Hone, Ralph E. *Dorothy L. Sayers: A Literary Biography*. Kent, Ohio: The Kent State University Press, 1979.

Jagger, Alison. "Political Philosophies of Women's Liberation." In *Feminism and Philosophy*, edited by Mary Vetterling-Braggin, Frederick A. Elliston, and Jane English, 5–21. Totowa, N.J.: Rowman and Littlefield, 1977.

Jennings, Bruce. "Tradition and the Politics of Remembering." *The Georgia Review* 36, no. 1 (Spring 1982): 167–82.

Kermode, Frank. *The Genesis of Secrecy: On the Interpretation of Narrative*. Cambridge, Mass.: Harvard University Press, 1979.

Ketchum, Sara Ann. "Liberalism and Marriage Law." In *Feminism and Philosophy*, edited by Mary Vetterling-Braggin, Frederick A. Elliston, and Jane English, 264–76. Totowa, N.J.: Rowman and Littlefield, 1977.

Lerner, Gerda. *The Creation of Patriarchy*. New York: Oxford University Press, 1986.

MacIntyre, Alasdair. *After Virtue*. Notre Dame, Ind.: University of Notre Dame Press, 1981.

Maison, Margaret. " 'Thine, Only Thine!' Women Hymn Writers in Britain,

1760–1835." In *Religion in the Lives of English Women*, edited by Gail Malmgreen, 11–40. Bloomington: Indiana University Press, 1986.

Malmgreen, Gail, ed. *Religion in the Lives of English Women*. Bloomington: Indiana University Press, 1986.

McAllister, Pam, ed. *Reweaving the Web of Life: Feminism and Nonviolence*. Philadelphia: New Society Publishers, 1982.

McKeon, Michael. *The Origins of the English Novel 1600–1740*. Baltimore: The Johns Hopkins University Press, 1987.

McWilliams-Tullberg, Rita. *Women at Cambridge*. London: Victor Gollancz Ltd., 1975.

Moore, Katherine. *Victorian Wives*. New York: St. Martin's Press, Inc., 1974.

Morrison, Toni. *Beloved*. New York: Alfred A. Knopf, 1987.

Morton, Nelle. *The Journey is Home*. Boston: Beacon Press, 1985.

Murray, Janet Horowitz. *Strong-Minded Women and Other Lost Voices from Nineteenth-Century England*. New York: Pantheon Books, 1982.

Perry, Ben Edwin. *The Ancient Romances*. Berkeley: University of California Press, 1967.

Peterson, M. Jeanne. "The Victorian Governess: Status Incongruence in Family and Society." In *Suffer and Be Still: Women in the Victorian Age*, edited by Martha Vicinus, 3–19. Bloomington: Indiana University Press, 1972.

Pickering, Samuel. *The Moral Tradition in English Fiction 1785–1850*. Hanover, N.H.: The University Press of New England, 1976.

Plaskow, Judith. *Sex, Sin and Grace: Women's Experience and the Theologies of Reinhold Niebuhr and Paul Tillich*. Lanham, Md.: University Press of America, 1980.

Prelinger, Catherine M. "The Female Deaconate in the Anglican Church: What Kind of Ministry for Women." In *Religion in the Lives of English Women*, edited by Gail Malmgreen, 161–92. Bloomington: Indiana University Press, 1986.

Raymond, Janice G. *A Passion for Friends: Toward a Philosophy of Female Affection*. Boston: Beacon Press, 1986.

Rees, Barbara. *The Victorian Lady*. London: Gordon & Crenonese, 1977.

Rich, Adrienne. *On Lies, Secrets and Silence*. New York: W. W. Norton & Company, 1979.

Rogers, Annie M. A. H. *Degrees by Degrees*. Great Britain: Oxford University Press, 1938.

Ruskin, John. "Of Queen's Gardens." In *Essays and Letters Selected from the Writings of John Ruskin*, edited by Mrs. Louis G. Hufford, 69–104. Boston: Ginn & Company, 1894.

Sampson, George. *The Concise Cambridge History of English Literature*. New York: The Macmillan Company, 1941.

Sandel, Michael J. "Morality and the Liberal Ideal." *The New Republic* (7 May 1984): 15–17.

Sayers, Dorothy L. *Are Women Human?* Grand Rapids, Mich.: William B. Eerdmans Publishing Company, 1971.

———. *Creed or Chaos?* New York: Harcourt, Brace and Company, 1949.

———. *Gaudy Night*. New York: Avon Books, 1968, Harper & Row Publishers Inc., 1936.

———. *The Mind of the Maker*. New York: Harcourt, Brace and Company, 1941.

———. *Unpopular Opinions*. New York: Harcourt, Brace and Company, 1947.

———. "Introduction." In Dante Alighieri, The Florentine, *The Comedy of Dante Alighieri*. Cantica II, *Purgatory* (*Il Purgatorio*), translated by Dorothy L. Sayers, 9–71. New York: Basic Books, Inc., Publishers, n.d.

Scholes, Robert, and Robert Kellogg. *The Nature of Narrative*. New York: Oxford University Press, 1966.

Shideler, Mary McDermott. "Introduction." In *Are Women Human?*, by Dorothy L. Sayers, 7–16. Grand Rapids, Mich.: William B. Eerdmans Publishing Company, 1971.

Shils, Edward. *Tradition*. Chicago: The University of Chicago Press, 1981.

Showalter, Elaine. *A Literature of Their Own*. Princeton, N.J.: Princeton University Press, 1977.

———. "Marriage Victorian-Style." Review of *The Bourgeois Experience*, by Peter Gay. *The Nation* 238 (24 March 1984): 356–59.

Snow, C. P. *The Masters*. New York: Charles Scribner's Sons, 1951.

Spacks, Patricia Meyer. *The Female Imagination*. New York: Alfred A. Knopf, 1975.

Sprague, Rosamond Kent, ed. *A Matter of Eternity: Selections from the Writings of Dorothy L. Sayers*. Grand Rapids, Mich.: William B. Eerdmans Publishing Company, 1973.

Stearns, Peter N. *Be A Man!* New York: Holmes & Meier Publishers, Inc., 1979.

Thurmer, John. *A Detection of the Trinity*. Exeter, England: The Paternoster Press, 1984.

Tischler, Nancy M. "Artist, Artifact and Audience: The Aesthetics and Practice of Dorothy Sayers." In *As Her Whimsey Took Her: Critical Essays on the Work of Dorothy L. Sayers*, edited by Margaret P. Hannay, 153–164. Kent, Ohio: The Kent State University Press, 1979.

————. *Dorothy L. Sayers: A Pilgrim Soul*. Atlanta: John Knox Press, 1980.

Trible, Phyllis. *Texts of Terror: Literary-Feminist Readings of Biblical Narratives*. Philadelphia: Fortress Press, 1984.

Vicinus, Martha, ed. *Suffer and Be Still: Women in the Victorian Age*. Bloomington: Indiana University Press, 1972.

Washington, Mary Helen, ed. *Invented Lives: Narratives of Black Women 1860–1960*. Garden City, N.Y.: Anchor Press, Doubleday & Company, Inc., 1987.

Watt, Ian. *The Rise of the Novel*. Berkeley: University of California Press; English Edition, London: Chatto and Windus Ltd., 1957.

Webster, Richard T. "*The Mind of the Maker*: Logical Construction, Creative Choice and the Trinity." In *As Her Whimsey Took Her: Critical Essays on the Work of Dorothy L. Sayers*, edited by Margaret P. Hannay, 165–75. Kent, Ohio: The Kent State University Press, 1979.

Weeks, Jeffrey. "An Anxious Sensibility." Review of *The Bourgeois Experience*, by Peter Gay. *History Today* 34 (August 1984): 54.

Wilenski, R. H. *John Ruskin: An Introduction to Further Study of His Life and Work*. New York: Russell & Russell, 1933.

Woolf, Virginia. *A Room of One's Own*. San Diego: Harcourt Brace Jovanovich, Publishers, 1929.

Young-Bruehl, Elisabeth. "The Education of Women as Philosophers." *Signs* 12, no. 2 (Winter 1987): 207–21.

Index

About the Author

Elizabeth A. Say is an Assistant Professor in the Department of Religious Studies, California State University, Northridge, teaching courses in Women and Religion and Feminist Ethics. She has a Ph.D. in Religious Social Ethics from the University of Southern California, with a particular emphasis in feminist theory and theology. Her current research interests include work on the development of a feminist methodology of narrative interpretation and theology (a continuation of work begun in this manuscript) and the reconceptualization of notions of the self as a basis for responsible ethical action.